'There is nothing like re̲[...]
ing honestly, openly, perso[...]
ing like this because it sel[...] ge of this
book breaks down stereotypes of what be[...] black man is . . . I
was inspired. I found hope.'   Benjamin Zephaniah

'We all know the narrative, images and media stories around
Black men often play to negative stereotypes, but in this collection, we see Black men re-writing those scripts to explore their
identities and their experiences in their own words. This anthology is utterly unique . . . I can't think of a book like it.'
                                                      Diane Abbott, MP

'This outstanding myth-busting book asks us to consider our
Black British brothers as individuals who are as multi-dimension-
al as the rest of the human race. Everyone should read it.'
                                                  Bernardine Evaristo

'This is not a book you read, but a book you witness. Derek
Owusu has brought together important voices in British culture,
authors you can actually feel digging deep into their experiences
and sharing things that have not been written before. It's brave
and honest, and not a moment too soon.'   Afua Hirsch

'A really eye-opening and vital book on the Black British male
experience.'   Matt Haig

'Black men have been reduced to stock one dimensional characters in the public imagination. This collection explodes those
myths, exploring the multi-hued textures of Black British masculinity in all its strength, vulnerability and diversity, providing an
intimate window into the lives beyond the statistics, the stereotypes and the headlines.'   Emma Dabiri

'A land   *Dazed*

SAFE

SAFE

20 Ways to be a
Black Man in Britain

Derek Owusu

First published in Great Britain in 2019 by Trapeze,
This paperback edition published in 2020 by Trapeze
an imprint of The Orion Publishing Group Ltd
Carmelite House, 50 Victoria Embankment,
London EC4Y 0DZ

An Hachette UK company

1 3 5 7 9 10 8 6 4 2

Introduction and *They May Not Mean to But They Do* © Derek Owusu 2018

Derek Owusu has asserted his right to be identified as the author of the introduction and
essay entitled *They May Not Mean to But They Do* in accordance with
the Copyright, Designs and Patents Act of 1988.

A CIP catalogue record for this book is
available from the British Library.

ISBN (Paperback): 978 1 409 18264 1

Typeset by Born Group

Printed and bound in Great Britain by Clays Ltd, Elcograf S.p.A.

www.orionbooks.co.uk

To **Yomi**,
whose integrity inspired me to do better and without whom
I wouldn't have learned to see the value in my own life.

And to **Berthy**,
who helped inspire my reading and whose friendship
and support has been unwavering.

Contents

Introduction
Is It True What They Say About Black Men?
Derek Owusu

You can find yourself on the London Underground. Among the throng of people with lineages that are left as answers to a question, your position becomes clear. What you thought you were, you are not. Every morning as I walk onto the Victoria line I'm reminded that there is something in the minds of commuters that makes me different and distant. They'd prefer an empty seat between, some distance from this foreign body. They may be worried for their possessions, thinking that, with the huge and much–desired part of me, I will somehow lift their valuables from them while both hands cup a book they're sure I'm not really reading. Once off the train, the journey up the escalator is no better: I can't stop behind anyone because my proximity is suspicious; I can't walk past too slowly, because that leaves time enough for me to take something from them. So I power-walk all the way up without a break, and put my good genes to use – remember it's all genetics. Such thoughts may seem paranoid and excessive, like someone with a slanted view because they're being weighed down by the chip on their shoulder, but I believe that these illuminate the subtle behaviours people would rather keep in the dark and also the thinking of someone who has experienced the micro-aggressions which lead to such caution.

Thousands of people pass us on public transport every day and I always feel that not one of them knows a true thing about me. They're content in what they think they know of the Black British male. Which is of course false, created by a legacy of racism, fear and ignorance. The inaccurate impressions and ideas about Black British men are everywhere. You find them on social media, on dating apps, in foster care, in interracial relationships, in the gym, and, often forgotten, in spaces traditionally occupied by Black people, like barbershops and our countries of origin.

All of the contributors to this anthology have relevant stories to tell, stories that were brought to life by seemingly harmless moments which could have occurred during trips from London Seven Sisters to Brixton. These 'minor' wounds grew until the only way to deal with them was to pour enough alcohol on them so that the screams let out could not be ignored.

We often make the mistake of thinking that people who hold damaging views about other people do no damage to themselves, are not diminishing their own humanity by being ignorant to the fact of others. I see writing is a way to heal – to not only heal the writer, but also the reader.

I've been looking for the Black British *Invisible Man*. I read the novel by Ralph Ellison at university and became obsessed with the paranoia, experiences and ideas of the nameless protagonist. That I connected so deeply with someone who was invisible tritely reveals truths about my own condition. In *Invisible Man*, Ellison captured not only something that was knowingly out of sight, but also something that was, at the time, also inaudible: the complex and complicated voice of African American people.

Because contemporary life, struggles and the history of Black men in Britain has been conflated with that of the African American male, it wasn't easy for me to see that I wasn't relating to Ellison's writing as Derek, a British-born Ghanaian, but as

Derek, a shadowy clone of the African American male experience. I was fixated on how these men lived, and so applied their grief and battles, all of which were conveyed to me through American literature, to my own life, without taking a look at the reality of the situation I was living in myself, a situation that also had a grief to be explored, albeit a more unspoken British kind. Many Black British males are stuck in this tragedy of being unseen and silent, and the best way, I believe, to help them out of it is to record their voice and play it back to them while a mirror reflects what they've failed to see, dismantling the myth that they, too, are invisible men.

Before I came to realise all this, my good friend Yomi Adegoke, a bastion of Black British culture, pointed out to me that there was a voice missing from the current conversation about diversity and representation. The two of us were sitting in a bar, arguing about something I was probably wrong about but too stubborn to admit to, when she expressed the thought that Black British males are not currently being given a platform on which to speak up, and because of this there was an audible silence slowly developing. I related because I had spent a lot of time trying to get my voice heard through my own literature podcast (my aim being to disrupt the common analyses of classics and inject them with some cultural relevance, while also pushing homegrown Black talent often ignored by the mainstream). I was starting to feel that there was something not quite right about some of the diverse books I was reading. Yomi explained that she felt that there needed to be multiple voices speaking at once, in harmony, about different lives and different experiences in the UK, otherwise the conversation she was now part of would be doing the very thing it was fighting against. So she made me responsible for gathering these voices and putting a microphone in front of them, and after few days of thinking about it and staring at my bookshelf, I accepted the challenge.

*

When you're a young Black boy, it's common to feel you must perform to be authentically Black – whatever that is. If you can't dance, for example, or if your speech lacks a certain rhythm and cadence, it's easy to feel out of time with the heartbeat of Black culture and identity. If you have no access to the perspectives and thoughts of Black British males, you're forced to accept what popular media, books and movies tell you about who you are and how you see the world. And, often, it's not even a Black British stereotype that is shoved down your throat: it's an African American one. The conflation is often subtle but once you realise the majority of things written and said about a Black man are really about the African American man, you wonder if you've *ever* been seen or heard.

Looking into literature and your surroundings and seeing yourself reflected back is life affirming. Black British pioneers such as Linton Kwesi Johnson, Paul Gilroy, Caryl Phillips and Sam Selvon set the pace for the discussions now taking place, and reflect both the potential achievements and the heights that contemporary young Black men know they can reach. These men spoke up and challenged racist Britain, took talk of diversity to a new plane, a plane that many Black males in Britain can now step on to in order to feel invigorated and speak freely. The peaks and troughs of the dialogue surrounding inclusion have been fluctuating since Olaudah Equiano put pen to paper in the eighteenth century, but now we're hearing that diversity is no longer a trend – that this time it's here to stay – so it's only right that *we* continue what was started long before we had experiences to speak of. It is my hope that this anthology will function as a mirror, a new conversation and a bridge.

This is a book I needed as a young boy, a teenager and a man, so I hope it can help men like myself and others who may not yet recognise their similarity to the Black men they share the world with.

I hope this anthology shatters the widely held opinions about Black men in the UK, and enables the reader to rebuild their views more carefully, based on what is learned about Black British men as individuals within this book. This book asks the reader to face themselves, their beliefs, the institutions they trust, and to take a seat next to a Black man and feel comfortable with the journey.

The F-word
Yomi Sode

Worn out, embarrassed and pretty much fed up of the mistreatment, Tina Turner decides to listen to her gut instinct and leave her husband, Ike. I remember the scene from the biopic vividly. The speed she got out of the bed to wake the kids, getting them dressed, frantically trying to hold composure while on the phone to her mother, the *Jesus, Jesus* in realizing the enormity of this decision. She leaves on the coach, not looking back, only to arrive at the destination with Ike already waiting for her. I watch on as Tina runs towards Ike, who now has the kids in the car, screaming for them to get out, but she's too late. A stand-off happens in the rain where she's left with little choice but to *get in the car.* At weddings, my father and mother would stand and join the other invited guests in welcoming the bride and groom. At some point during the joyful proceedings of the day, my father would say to my mother, *'This could be you, if you . . .'*. What came after the *'if you'* is not important, but I believe it cemented her worth in the relationship. It was as constant as a reoccurring dream, or nightmare. Like Tina, one day the coin dropped for Mum. Ask me what the drop was for Tina and I couldn't tell you, but having a piece of cake shoved in your face against your will in front of friends and family definitely ranks up on the list of fucked-up things to do. While Dad was no Ike, he still did enough to convince her the end was nigh.

Nine years old. Mum woke me up the night she decided to leave my father. I walked into the living room seeing uncles and aunties moving the last parts of our belongings out of the house. I remember the silence when packing our things and their hushed tones when speaking. Unlike Tina, this was a plan in the making for over nine months. Unlike Ike, my father returned to an empty home that evening, then (with family in tow) stormed to my grandmother's compound shouting 'Where is she! Where is my son?' repeatedly, but no wall, dog, ceiling fan or grandmother uttered a word.

Weeks earlier, Mum entered my nine-year-old self to star in a Nigerian version of Different Strokes. This was 1992, the year the Nigerian Olympic team travelled to Barcelona to compete, the year that mourned sixty people in the Zango Kataf riots and the year that I was destined for the stage. In talking further about this years later, Mum recalls my excitement regarding the role, how I made it through to the final audition despite other mothers apparently trying to bribe their way or sabotage my chances. We rehearsed the lines every night before bedtime to get it right but, unfortunately, I left Nigeria on the day of the final audition. She said I cried on the way to the airport, staring out of the window, wanting to return. Even years later as we joke about it, I felt the sting of her decision them many years back. Call me stupid but I expected a sorry, or something. But I got nothing.

I process the F-word as a strenuous task. A muscle one has to work to strengthen. I start most days far from gym-ready, but still expecting to lift what's in front of me. Martin Luther King, Jr shared a thought regarding the F-word:

'We must develop and maintain the capacity to Forgive. He who is devoid of the power to Forgive is devoid of the power to love.'

It's December 2005. Earlier that year, I was attacked at work after being in the way of a gang, foiling their orchestrated plan to ambush one of my young people, and my face, body and family experienced the wrath of their anger. Needing a break, Mum and I flew to Jacksonville, Florida, staying in the suburbs with my Aunty.

Jacksonville, Florida is very white. The B-side to what I thought was a stop-off on our way to Miami. It is my first time in America, all channels are filled with Chris Brown launching, 'Excuse me Miss' to the world. Oddly enough, I notice the water flowing in the toilet is much higher to the toilets in London. Dad calls me that evening, the conversation dry and time-consuming until he tells me to hold, then hands the phone over to two girls, aged eight and thirteen. I later find out that they are my half-sisters. Elated, I run to tell Mum who has this awkward reaction to my excitement. The evening sets in and I hear muffled sniffles from the passage. I follow the sound to find Mum crying on her bed – my mother never cries. The last time I remember her crying was in Nigeria when her grandmother died.

He had children and did not tell us, he is married and did not tell us. She is angry, the type of anger that triggers a memory of attending weddings and being told how to behave in order to be a wife, a triggered memory of keeping silent when food is disposed of in favour of another. I felt the excitement drain out of me and my capacity to Forgive for her wore thin.

I am thirty-something now, exploring the F-word and struggling to make sense of it. Holding on to emotions tighter than any bag clutched in public spaces where Black folks are present and almost using it as fuel to keep my energy the way it is, a justification, so to speak. It's like having the strongest belief system and something happening to a loved one or you that leads you to notice its flaws, leaving you unsure as to how or what to believe any more.

So I've been looking into mindfulness. Mindfulness leads me to realise that, frustratingly, I have internalised so much for the best part of my life, for fear of getting something wrong or upsetting people. When I was thirteen, I remember being locked in a school with a group of kids and adults due to a disturbance outside. When given the all clear, we are rushed to the coach to take us home. En route home, I look out and spot these white teenagers making monkey noises and sounds, I laugh, thinking, *what are they doing?* I look at the staff member wanting to share the joke. I look at him, a brown face like mine that's not laughing, *why aren't you laughing,* I think to myself. Years later, I realise why he wasn't laughing or maybe he was – at me, in thinking how lost I must have been to not see or get it.

Late 2013: it's literally five minutes before I start proceedings to a show I have been booked to host. The space is rammed with excited young people and teenagers, some high off the free sweets. I'm there to control the levels of crazy throughout this two-hour shindig. The booker approaches before the show officially kicks off, handing me a sheet of paper: *'Emma is not going to read so I thought you could do it on her behalf. It reads like a rap, you should know what that's like, right?'*

I can't explain what happened after she said it. I know my face spoke louder than my voice did, the staff standing beside us, me, noticed. Silenced, we watched on as she walked off gracefully as though the movie is ending with its happy ever after, then snapped back to reality with, *'I am so sorry that she said that!'* But it's too late.

In 'Strangers', Kano pens a song addressing a broken relationship with an old friend. A song balancing the tightrope of vulnerable and man in equal measure. He raps:

Seven years ago was Shane's little one's christening / AB was there tryna put to bed all the bickering / He made a phone call to you in the toilets / Said 'someone wants to speak', gave me the phone to my annoyance / I said 'hello?', you must've heard my voice and hung up / I just heard the phone cut out and picked my rum up / And hit the dancefloor to some Mavado, finger gun up / Water off a duck's back, but truth be told, that hurt, my brother.

I imagine Kano skanking his hurt out on the dancefloor, the same way my amped voice reluctantly read the poem handed to me before girl and audience. Each stanza feeling like a stabbing, triggering the coach trip, the look on the brown staff member's face and deeper anger towards my parents for not prepping me regarding racism, slavery, white privilege / ignorance because they were fixed on themselves and their relationship instead. Knowing how different my outlook would be if I was equipped with this knowledge.

I have had more confrontations in the last four years than I can remember. A purging of sorts to get to the core of the relationships around me. At one point, I felt as though songs were speaking directly to me! Wretch 32's 'Grown on Me': *'Aware of the responsibilities, grown on me, And when I wear a suit and tie it looks grown on me, I ain't changed, I'm just a new old me, Or did you know me?'*

14 December 2013. Family members and friends were handed fortune cookies while waiting for their meal to be served. This wasn't only a celebration of my birthday, it would also be a future they never saw coming. It sounded like a ripple of crackling knuckles followed with gasps and *what!* and looks of bewilderment. The paper inside the fortune cookie read, *'We're having a baby'.* Mum, finally clocking on past the screams and congratulations charges towards us in full glory, I am sure our first in-

stinctual calling in protecting our child started at this point. Ten minutes before the unveiling, I was outside calling my cousin, seeing how far he was. Everyone was here bar him. Eight rings and two voicemails later, I stopped calling and made my way inside to make the announcement. When I was fourteen, this same cousin took me under his wing and introduced me to his family. He didn't have to; he was older and even now I still wonder why. I had a flat top then due to idolising Mike Tyson and Christopher 'Play' Reid's haircuts and my cousin put an end to that. Taking me to the manor's local barber to trim it all off. A short back and sides trim, a genesis of my adolescense. Early experiences of masculinity came through him. Driving and crashing cars, speaking to girls, attending raves, being in life-threatening situations, all through him. The closest thing I had to a Sidney Deane, Sonny, Mike Lowrey. Nothing connecting us by blood but we were as good as related.

Four days after my son's first birthday, I message him asking what I have done to upset him, not knowing whether I had done anything at all. I guess the undertone of that message to him was how a year could go by and my boy lay his eyes on everyone close to me but him. His response was simple. *'We have outgrown each other, we lead different lives, I wish you the best.'*

A year later, our paths cross at a family gathering. It felt like an awkward break-up in which you both still share friends and are forced to be at the same place. As you would imagine, my petty kicked in so high, one would think I was the fucking Shard reimagined in Nigerian greatness. Through careful constructing of family, though, we reconnected. He apologised and we spent three days away to catch up. He met my boy (several times), and six months later he did it again.

2018 marks two years since we last spoke. Maybe it's being a father now that means it has bugged me more than it should, or knowing the amount of love I can invest in another that makes this hard to get over. It's like I am an AI trying to make sense of forgiveness and acceptance, all the while feeling hurt by the abruptness in leaving and not explaining why.

Should I attempt to write out all my situations on Post-it notes and stick them on my wall, I'll soon realise that this act of the F-word comes with its fair share of ownership and self-indulgence.

1 May 2018, I stop by Rich Mix to order a Lamb Bhuna with rice, paratha and a Coke. I then join the millions worldwide on You-Tube to tune into Charlemagne the God's interview with Kanye West. Kanye (of some sound mind) talks through his thinking, ideologies, irks and, of course, tours his apparel and acres upon acres of land. The irony of course in Ye being Ye is all that Ye hears or talks about – is Ye. While all of my angst towards and from others is internalised and in some way being purged, I start to also explore my intention. Did I go into something expecting a return? Am I being selfless enough? Am I being attentive to what they may be going through?

January 2015, one of my closest friends was remanded for an un-provoked attack towards a man. Police found him at the scene drunk, his knuckles swollen and bloodied. He was charged with murder later that year and sentenced to life in prison with no pa-role and I am angry because that is not my friend of twenty-plus years. I sit through visits not discussing the elephant in the room. I go weeks before deciding to write a letter. It feels as though I stopped caring but I know I haven't. I am sad that he is in there in the same way he is sad that I have to visit him there.

This journey of mindfulness. The NHS have a blurb regarding how it works. *It's about allowing ourselves to see the present moment clearly. When we do that, it can positively change the way we see ourselves and our lives* and truth is, making something present means you're faced with something you probably won't like. So, here's me holding a mirror to myself asking whether it's me that needs to be purged of the anger first in order to see things clearly, then realising that though I wasn't raised around as much chaos – there has been a history of harbouring happening in my life.

Many moons ago my mother left my father in what I can only describe as an *Ocean's* 8-type execution that left him emasculated and alone. I doubt my father has forgiven her. There's this man thing regarding pride that would rather struggle underwater than rise to the surface for breath. I go further to add the specific type of stubbornness worn by an African man that I've grown to know. The kind that will get married and have children that soon grow their own animosity. The kind that'll watch his grandson grow to be four without a call to wish him happy birthday, not once. My father is still hurting after all these years and his children and grandchildren are paying the price. I remember writing a three-page letter to him when I was younger. The letter was a plea to him and our relationship, my willingness to work if he, too, was willing to work. His response was one page that addressed my grammatical errors, nothing else, and that never left me. My mother saw him last in 2016 and described how frail he looked. My Grandma begs me to forgive him and carry on as normal and this is where culture favours people like my father; it knows how to act like something never happened even if you know it did, how to rotate a lens to draw focus on you being problematic, too much ego to let go or too vulnerable to be affected.

In the climactic scene of Natasha Gordon's play *Nine Night* [SPOILER ALERT], the spirit of Gloria (Mum) enters Aunty Maggie (Gloria's cousin) and begins to share parting words with Trudy (Gloria's eldest daughter), Robert (Trudy's half-brother) and Uncle Vince (Maggie's husband), but leaves out Lorraine

(Trudy's half-sister and Gloria's main carer in the lead up to her death). The spirit then begins to ascend to the heavens by way of the back door; Lorraine holds a knife to whoever dares to open the door until Gloria shares a message with her in the same way she did with the others. But Lorraine does not get the message. Despite sleepless nights and quitting her job to care for her mother when no one else was around, her search for some acknowledgement never happens. The back door is opened and Gloria's spirit leaves.

In my case, my father could die tomorrow and I'd be left worse off than when I started. I wrote a whole play regarding the relationship with my mother because deep down a conversation was harder to have in person. The initial draft was so raw I'm sure it bled. Writing it over and over, pretty much like this essay, marked the dropping of my coin. If forgiveness had a voice it would also be in this conundrum channelling its inner Ye, screaming, *You don't have the answers, Yomi!* – and maybe I don't. Maybe I just have to step out of myself and look at the situation in its entirety.

August 2018, I'm startled at the sight of an old friend in ASDA when I have my son in hand. Her daughter is not too far from her. This marks eleven years since we last spoke. Walking past each other felt painful especially as we are now both parents. Thinking back, a conversation could have sorted it out, maybe. A conversation that'd then lead to us reflecting on the years wasted due to misunderstandings. I should have spoken to her that afternoon at the supermarket, but my reason not to boiled down to pride – a fear of being embarrassed, as opposed to just breaking the silence because it felt right and outside of this manifested bubble. The fact that we are both alive and well was worthy of celebration, and how easily traits such as pride can be passed on to our children.

The F-word, forgiveness, is a mixing board I've had little control over. Its channels (pride, vulnerability, selfishness, etc.) are sometimes turned high, skewing the levels and requiring the engineer in me to better mix the noise for clarity. Forgiveness is something I still battle with. Whether it's with myself or others.

They May Not Mean To But They Do

Derek Owusu

I've always thought anyone able to look at my life's script would have seen this coming from the first act; would have easily concluded where my life was headed after reading the first conflict. God, the author of my life, was penning a tragedy when my character came to him. I was put between four walls with my arms tied up, passive to everything that came my way. I was splintering, cracking, taking everything the world could throw at me, destined to shatter and reflect the cruel mind of a God who hated his own image. But no destiny is fixed and with time I was able to take control, claim the space I was supposed to die in and make it my own. I reshaped it, reached outside of it and allowed others to help me live. And now that this is my story and no longer a tragedy but a tale of hope, I'd like to share it with you. From the very beginning.

I was twelve months old when the first of a few broken hearts happened. My mum was twenty-five, hoping to become British and newly single. The love story of her life, which had started on the Victoria line, as she ran for the train doors and my dad held them open, had come to an end. She was still in love, a lonely type of love, the Just-Arrived-Ghanaian in London type of love, which isn't born from a desire to be held for ever, but from the immediate relatability and cultural oneness of two immigrants trying to make a better life in the Western world. My dad was wealthy, mildly attractive, from the same village as her and had citizenship. My mum had nothing and wanted my father, which is probably what attracted him to her. For a little while.

The argument that ended it all still plays in the back of my mind like a song I haven't heard for years but fight to hold on to the fading melody. I was one. Voices were raised, doors were slammed, and I was given some fruit to calm my distress. Soon after, my father left me and my mother for what he thought was an even better life, and I can't imagine him feeling any turbulence or disturbance as he reclined in his seat and closed his eyes, leaving his son behind as he flew over the Atlantic. When he landed in New York, I wasn't to hear from him again for eleven years. Straight after his departure, my mum having little money and single black women receiving scarcely any support, I was put in foster care. My mum maintains that it was a difficult decision because, at the time, the early 90s, it was the only choice she had that didn't end with us both living on the street. At twelve months old, my bond with my mother would have been strong, and this rupturing, which left me with a white mother and living in a small village in Suffolk, would have sent shockwaves through my soft body and begin to harden what would later become a confused identity.

And then I'm seven years old. I've read a few articles describing children as young as five as having depression. And growing up in care is often a variable. But I can't say that this was a narrative that belonged to me. I loved foster care, loved my foster mum and thought Long Melford, Suffolk, was where I'd grow up and spend my old days with my friends, moaning, grumbling, and taking walks in wellingtons to the melody of *Last of The Summer Wine*. Watching my foster mother plucking the feathers off a pheasant she'd picked up on a drive, the strict structure of the meals – breakfast, dinner and tea time – the fruit picking, the jelly making, the harvest festival and especially the Christmases – all of this was heaven to a younger me who was unknowingly a visitor in a world that didn't belong to him.

My real mum visited every few months and although I had a vague idea of who she was, I didn't take much notice of her. I would accept the attention she gave me but never internalise it to the point of building a fondness for her or the beginnings of a relationship. As young as I was, there was something within me that understood that if this was my real mother, then she had abandoned me and given up her chance to love me. Now and then, I would be asked by my foster parents or biological mother if I wanted to take a trip with her. Sometimes I wouldn't mind but other times I would be repulsed by the idea, as though I had forgotten who she was and only recognised her as the woman who sat and stared at me as I played, never talking to me, but frowning whenever I got a little too rough with my toys. On these trips, we travelled to London a few times, visiting cousins and the local council – I hated the council part of my trips to London because I had to sit down and keep quiet while my mum cried in front of a clerk sitting behind the glass window. Because of these infrequent trips, I wasn't surprised when my real mum and I got on a train heading into the capital. I can't remember what I was thinking about but I do recall catching my mum looking at me with her lips pressed tightly together and her brow furrowed, as if she were angry at what was inevitably going to be my reaction to what she was planning to tell me.

'You're not going back there.'

I didn't react because, what was she talking about?

'Hey, Kwesi, you're not going back there. You're coming to live with me.'

I knew she was talking to me but I didn't know who Kwesi was. Later on, I realised it was my Ghanaian name, a name and identity lost to me until then. I said nothing in response. When we arrived in London, we travelled round to all of my cousins' houses – greeting was customary, so we made our way around Tottenham like the newly arrived at a Ghanaian gathering, shaking hands with all the attendees already sitting. We ate, what I thought at the time, was strong-smelling and spicy food, expected to dip my bare hands, clutching a farina and mash mix, into the soup. After the meal, I noticed the darkness and wondered about the time we'd be leaving, when my mum asked if I wanted to sleep on the floor or the bed. Then it happened. A build-up I had been ignoring suddenly burst out of my body and my limbs began flailing. I don't remember how long I was screaming, kicking, punching and crying. But I know I slept on the floor for the next four months. I had lost another mother. And the sobs I soaked into the sheet laid upon the carpet took away my speech and I said nothing during that period until the council offered us a house and my mum offered me a bed.

So now we had our own space. But while we lived at number 60 Truelock Court, I still remained within my four walls, hardening and cracking at the same time. My mother and I began to fight daily. I'm sure I was being 'disciplined' for what my father had done and I could see an older reflection of myself in my mum's eyes every time she raised her hand to hit me. During this time I wanted to be away from her. I'd always ask to go to a cousin's house and then sit alone with my thoughts or toys. I spoke to my toys. They were my friends and berated my mother for the way she was treating me. In a way, they found their way into my space, sitting against a wall with me, silently consoling, their heads resting on my hips. Many parents think there is nothing wrong with hitting their children, putting them in their place and showing them who the adult is. But in my opinion, if you feel you need to show your child how grown you are by putting your hands on them, then you shouldn't be a parent. Being emotionally damaged or power hungry and raising a child is a combination that will only end in tragedy.

My dad returned from New York when I was eleven and my entire family thought it was my dreams coming into reality. But by morning my dreams were always forgotten and there wasn't ever any attempt at recollection. Everyone was excited – a secret was being forced back by the grinning teeth of everyone who knew. I've never had so many relatives smiling at me. I was aware of what was coming because I understood Twi but pretended I didn't. I had never really longed for my dad to return, but I knew there was some sort of status attached to having a mum and a dad so I welcomed his homecoming. '*Akwaaba*'. It was theatrical. There was a knock on my aunt's door and I was told to go downstairs and open it (the flats in Broadwater Farm, Tottenham, where my aunt lived were upside-down). When I opened the door, my Uncle Dave was stood in front of me with a stiff smile. 'GotASur-prise,' he forced out of his pursed lips. And then HAH, my dad stepped out in front of him with a smile on his face as if he'd made my day. Had I developed my adult mannerism at that time I would have demurely said, 'You all right, yeah?' But instead, I said nothing. They both probably thought I was shocked. My dad picked me up and bounced me a few times like I was the child he had left behind. Ten years had passed. My friend, you're too late.

My dad came and went, and slowly he became David. The transition from filial respect to first-name basis went unnoticed and by the time I was fourteen I struggled to dredge up any respect for this man who treated our house like a hotel and carried himself like a lodger in the home that was supposed to belong to his family. Our relationship was non-existent but I never went so far as to outright disrespect him. He was still my dad and, as a child, I still experienced a slight thrill and sense of pride when I made him happy. But that wasn't often. David had a way with his hands. His feints and jabs would send my thoughts back to Suffolk and better times. My foster dad was a gentle and calm man. He dragged his feet when he walked, the sole of his slipper rough against all surfaces, so we always knew when he was coming. And he took his time, sometimes five minutes to walk from his garage to the living room. He was a lot older than my foster mother and a lot weaker. I used to give him head rubs, scratching my nailless fingers over his bald head while he relaxed and told me stories of Sinbad. He never raised a hand to me. So I was heartbroken that the rough hand wiping tears was now replaced by the one that caused them.

Most of my punishments I can't remember, but the one that has stayed with me, and made me question my place in the world and my sanity, is a slap David gave me, I thought, unfairly. In the afternoon my cousins had come over and, when they were leaving, I pointed my finger at them. It wasn't serious – I was sad they were leaving so I did whatever came to mind to engage with them as they left. When they got home they told their mother I stuck my middle finger up at them and this was then relayed back to my mum. My mum told my dad and when he got home from work I was told to stand still in front of him. I had no idea what I had done and was thinking that some bad news was going to be broken to me gently. A few seconds passed and then my dad slapped me across the face as hard as he could. I fell to the floor with my cheek burning and my head spinning. Confused, I looked to my mum for help but she gave me that look, the look from the train with her lips tight and her brow furrowed. She was angry at me too and had no sympathy. I crawled away, crying. I heard my dad saying something along the lines of: because of my rudeness, my aunt won't let the kids come here again. I reached the kitchen and headed to the back door. It was night-time. I sat down on the stoop and looked up at the darkness and stars. I had never seen them before. I appreciated them. I wondered how long they would last and how long I would last. One day, I and the stars would die. Death was real. And suddenly, so was I.

I hadn't heard from my foster mum in years. It didn't bother me too much because back when I lived with her there were seven other children in the house. She was busy, and if she was still doing what she'd done with us, there would be no time to think about Derek. Up until the age of fourteen, I had visited Suffolk for Christmas. Ghanaians don't really celebrate Christmas and I'm sure my mum was happy to be rid of me because I was becoming troublesome. But then suddenly I stopped going. Honestly, I barely noticed. I was getting older and other things preoccupied my mind. But I did think of her. I was now turning into a young man and often wondered what she would think of who I was becoming. She could have reassured me that it would all make sense soon, that my feeling shut out by my family's culture and ignored by my adopted one was just a phase and that soon I would know where I stood, even if the chewing gummed pavement seemed shaky. These musing were around the time my mum and I argued constantly. The beatings from her had stopped but there were still screams, but this time from the both of us. We'd argue over the smallest things, growing so sick of each other that any minor issue was a reason for a fight. The house we lived in had two bedrooms and because my dad, strangely, didn't want to sleep in the same bed with my mum, I took his place. This is where most of the arguments would happen and during a particularly heated one my mum, thinking of the best way to hurt me, shouted out, 'June is dead.'

June, my foster mum, was dead. I can still feel how I felt then.

'How could she die? How could you tell me like this?' I cried. I wailed. I hurt. 'You left me again, June, and you betrayed me again, Mum.' Though mother's expression after those words was unfamiliar, I could sense the regret but couldn't feel the warmth she hoped to comfort me with when she put her hand on my shoulder. Nothing radiated. I was cold. And so here I am.

I was numb then but I now feel intensely. But the numbness I can summon, ask to dull an emotion I don't want to feel or that I can't control. It's why I can cut myself so easily, watch my skin split and the white flesh slowly appear like the back of a shark rising out of the Black Sea. These events have made me who I am, made me no one and everyone. I'm every emotion, felt so acutely in the moment that I become them. But beneath it all, I struggle to see who I really am. In my calmest moments, I am the most lost. But although I, no, we, have been shaped, by the events that pull us apart before hardening us into something almost unbreakable, we can learn to throw the clay and turn our space into the Potter's House. I learned that through my tears I was softening the material I'm made from, making myself more vulnerable, malleable to change. I realised that my story, all our stories, are about transformation and creation. And that's why I'm here, talking to you. I grew tired of pretending that the slight feeling of hope I feel isn't enough, enough to drive me forward and away from a self-inflicted death. Yes, I believe hope is enough, and as long as we cling to it, the only direction it can take us is up, up out of the mess we've allowed to consume us. I'm rambling. I've been talking a lot and you haven't said much. That's how it starts, she said. You say everything you feel you need to, and then we unpack it all. How do you feel now? I actually feel a bit better. It felt good to get all that out. Well, there's twenty minutes left of our session. I don't have another client after this so why don't we spend the next thirty minutes trying to dissect what I feel are the key points in what you've told me? OK.

Why It Is Important for Young Black Men to Floss (Not Their Teeth)

Suli Breaks

floss

flɒs/

verb

gerund or present participle: **flossing**

1. clean between (one's teeth) with dental floss.

2. US *informal*

behave in a flamboyant manner; show off.

I can guarantee you that at this precise moment, there is a child in a council estate somewhere in London, face contorted in focus, fingers and hand worn from effort and determination.

He's hunched over on a mattress that squeaks desperately under the weight of his abrupt movements.

In one hand, he has a toothbrush, holding it the same way a sculptor holds a chisel, or a builder a hammer, and in the other hand, one shoe of a pair. The shoe is more than likely branded by one of the top three labels that have dominated youth culture since the early 80s, Nike, Adidas or Reebok. With the toothbrush, he is scrubbing meticulously, ensuring each bristle salvages and excavates every ounce of dirt which has managed to stain the soles of the shoes. It is a time-consuming and far from glamorous procedure, but he will scrub relentlessly for hours, then dip the brush in the soapy water at his feet, then scrub again.

Scrub, Dip, Scrub, Dip. Scrub Dip.

This rhythm has almost become the soundtrack for the young Black male experience. There is a constant pressure to adjust, polish, and present yourself in a specific way constantly. Wearing the same clothes more than once is a violation! Being out of fashion is taboo! The current trends almost dictate your every move.

It's a constant cycle – you always have to have the latest items, clothes, accessories and technology.

The pressure is a constant melody. People from the outside looking in may not appreciate the gravity of a young Black man's emphasis on personal appearance, but within our community how we looked, and what we wore, was everything that defined us. Many times, for us, it has felt like the difference between life and death.

Let me try and explain. Imagine, you come from a place where everybody is on government benefits, minimum wage. All your houses are the same unserviced, cramped, two-bedroomed flats. Basically, your living conditions have already predetermined your status and value. How do you separate yourself from everyone else?

Then to add to that, as a young Black male, you are constantly stereotyped by society, mainstream media has pretty much portrayed you in whichever light suits their current agenda.

Criminal. Thug. Troublemaker, Aggressive, Rebel . . . Poor.

How do you disassociate yourself from these labels?

*

WHY IT IS IMPORTANT FOR YOUNG BLACK MEN TO FLOSS (NOT THEIR TEETH)

Every social group has to deal with being stereotyped. Stereotypes, you almost become accustomed to or at least learn to tolerate. What becomes hard to accept is being *'defined'*. This is someone not only determining your current status, but more harmfully dictating the extent of your potential, deciding your destiny.

One of the most basic aspects of human nature is to want to believe that you have control over your future. Everybody wants to be given the opportunity to define themselves. To tell their story, in a way they feel truly represents them.

One thing about Black people: we have always prided ourselves on being resourceful. In the most demeaning situations, we have always found ways to tell our own personal stories. Examples of slaves in bondage creating songs to not only articulate their struggle, but also to communicate messages of liberation and secrets to their peers, are numerous. Storytelling has always had significance with the Black community, and we have always strived to tell our own unique ones, whether it be through sports, music, and in the case of 'flossing', fashion! Flossing almost became a way to define our identities.

The kid strokes the brush over his trainers one final time then cautiously holds them to sunlight that has managed to creep its way through his window. He admires his work. The last thirty minutes have been worth it. He then crosses the room to his wardrobe; he takes a deep breath and levers the wardrobe wide open. Inside it are rows of attire, with exchange values of considerably more than anything a majority of his peers or his family could afford. He owns jackets the price of his mother's monthly earnings, shirts that could pay their weekly rent two times over. He sees himself as no different from the more privileged members of society. Yet, while as children they opened wardrobes and dreamed off passages to new worlds, he found ways to fill his with multiples paths to a new reality. He gently thumbs through his options, the rhythm is the same.

Growing up as a young Black man in north London, I saw flossing was a way to tell your story. High-end, branded clothes meant wealth and success. Imitations and knock-offs indicated struggle and disadvantage. The concept is really simple if you think about; in an environment where everybody pretty much owned nothing, you prioritised gestures or practices that explicitly show you had something. People may think flashy watches and big chains were limited to representations of ego and extravagance, whereas in reality, they were also a way for a person to distinguish his personality from another.

Flossing helped to establish a hierarchy. Thinking about it now, our parents adhered to this same standard, but in a subtler yet more formal way. Growing up, it wasn't unusual to see older African men, who worked in what most would consider menial service industries, wearing the most extravagant shoes, combined with loud, stylish (at least, by their standard) suits, accessorised with gleaming imitations of popular watch and glasses brands. I had uncles who were cleaners and security guards, but would be dressed like politicians and government delegates on Sundays. In the same manner, aunties would be dressed in hand-tailored traditional clothing of the highest standard.

It was no doubt to convince their peers and community that they were people of status and commanded the same respect as the figures they were attempting to emulate. So, there was almost a hereditary nature to a *flossing mentality*.

However, for young Black men, status symbols in our community were not related to politics or figures in academia; we admired sports stars and musicians who consistently expressed their wealth through a glamorous relationship with fashion and luxury items. Having the latest trainers that you had seen someone wear in a music video or a chain/watch meant you were somebody! It gave you an identity; it showed your peers and members of the opposite sex that you were 'the man' in your community.

WHY IT IS IMPORTANT FOR YOUNG BLACK MEN TO FLOSS (NOT THEIR TEETH)

It's interesting to talk about the dual relationship of celebrities and flossing in the community. When you think about it, the celebrities, especially rappers, often come from similar environments to the demographic they attempt to make their music resonate with. So they are inherently aware of the significance of flossing. In some way, they are forced to acknowledge that the only way their audience will buy into their brand or persona is if they continually invest in flossing to further emphasise their 'success'. It is not uncommon for artists to rent cars, houses, jewellery or even girls they can't afford for music videos to create a perception their audience can respect. The sad irony is that in doing this they further perpetuates the idea to people that they need all the same things their favourite artist has 'rented' to represent their own success. It has then become a vicious cycle, with both sides of the community putting pressure on the other to adhere to sometimes unrealistic standards.

He checks his reflection twice in the mirror in his room, then goes into his mum's room so he can use the full-length one. He feels something is off. Something doesn't feel right. The outfit feels too . . . familiar. He frantically takes his phone out of his pocket, ignorant to the barrage of requests on the screen requiring an update on his status.

'Where are you fam?

'How long are you going to be?

'Bruv, pick up?!'

He finally reaches the target of the search, an Instagram post on his account. Two weeks ago. He has his arms around an attractive female, leaning into him, while he poses holding a bottle, filled with the remnants of some alcoholic beverage of extreme value. He recognises the source of his initial familiarity, and erupts internally!

The outfit the version of himself in the photo is wearing is an exact replica of the collection he is wearing today.

'Fuck!'
He races back into his bedroom to begin the routine again.

Flossing has been our way as young Black males to establish our identity and assert our status within our communities. In every community, status is always indicated by the way people are treated and by their quality of living. The more affluent and enriched members of society are well respected and adored. Those with less are often mistreated and dismissed. These dynamics have different implications depending on your society. I remember being in Mumbai, India, and the poorest members of society lined the streets, desperate and neglected. As a foreigner, to me it was disturbing, but the natives walked past unfazed: it was the norm. That was how it was in that society if you were poor or underprivileged: your life was of less value and so was your standard of living.

We experienced a similar dynamic in inner-city London. Basically, the better and more established you looked, the less likely you were to be stigmatised, bullied, shunned. Brand-new cars or clothes meant that you were someone of value, or you at least valued your personal status enough to understand the response it commanded.

Flossing also helped in some way to establish a common ground and understanding. It wasn't unusual that once a certain hat or bag came into fashion, every kid on the bus would be camouflaged against each other with the same style. Almost as if it was uniform! In a way, that conformity created a sense of unity and security.

On the flipside of that, the practice of being too obvious or apparent with your flossing made you a victim for people to want to take what you have. Outsiders would describe it as criminal and greedy. However, growing up we saw it as something normal. I almost used to see it as natural, in the same way as the human body reacts to a virus. Vaccinations are basically the process of injecting some of a virus into your body to encourage your immune system to act. In a similar way, when people see someone who makes them uncomfortable or feel lower in status they may attempt to re-establish the status quo. This more often than not results in numerous attempts to embarrass the person exhibiting what they would consider a disproportionate amount of affluence and success. Of course, this is mainly to satisfy their own criminal desires, egos, and insecurities, so I cannot justify such action. Yet there are self-appointed people who provide a such a function within the community. People most of us made sure to avoid. This was one of the negative outcomes of drawing attention to yourself.

Similarly, not being up to date on the latest trends and styles – basically not flossing! – could also make you victim, but on more of an emotional level, causing you to be shunned, isolated, ostracised and subjected to humiliation. It almost became an exercise in preserving your mental health by simply choosing to conform for peace of mind.

Conclusively, it would be too easy to assume flossing is a by-product of pride and ego. Yet if the surface layer is stripped back and you look at the underlying implications and impact of these practices, you understand the relationship they share with the basic concepts of expression, identity and survival. Young Black men have learned to use flossing as a means to navigate an environment within which they are given very few tools or options to create an identity and establish their self-worth.

He takes a final glance in the mirror, analyses his entire composition as he takes an extravagant watch face from a shelf above his closest and plants it majestically on his wrist. He runs through the checklist in his head; the effort, the focus, the time have been invested wisely. As his peers would say, he looks like money. Which means, he looks nothing like his overdue phone bill and car insurance, his pending over-

time required to afford his luxuries and the rent money he will be short on when his mother asks for it again this month. In essence, he looks nothing like his reality. He is dressed to represent who he wants to be, and what he wants to embody, rather than what his environment and society is attempting to restrict him to. These clothes and jewellery are not just for fashion, they represent potential and opportunity. He closes the cupboard door and heads downstairs, tiptoeing over each step, to prevent a crease forming on the front of the trainers he is wearing.

As he approaches the front door to leave his house, he takes one last look at his reflection in the window and smiles proudly; he smooths over a bristle in his jacket, straightens the position of his T-shirt underneath his jumper and heads for the exit. He takes a deep breath and turns the knob. With little hesitation, he swings the door open and steps outside. His clothes, his style, his swag give him confidence; he's a man, he's a person. Not just another poor Black boy in a low-income council estate. He's whoever he wants to be. Now he's ready to face the world.

Scrub, Dip, Scrub, Dip. Scrub Dip.

What's in a Name?

Alex 'Reads' Holmes

I am obsessed with names.

As a young boy, calling names was a part of life. The things we call people inevitably leave a mark, but as I grew older, I realised that names were more than just words. Some may call them a blessing, while some may consider them a burden.

This is the conundrum I find myself in. Is my name a blessing or a burden? What is in a name? Does it carry the cultural impact we desire? Should it be held in such high regard? What is it that makes a name so powerful, important and somewhat prophetic when applied to African and Caribbean people?

My name has no influential or spiritual meaning in either British or Caribbean culture. It is just a name. In researching my name, I found:

Greek Meaning:
The name Alexander is a Greek baby name. In Greek, the meaning of the name Alexander is: defender of men.

Alexander the Great was a fourth-century Macedonian king for whom the Egyptian city of Alexandria is named. Eight popes and three Russian emperors have been named Alexander.

Biblical Meaning:
The name Alexander is a Biblical baby name.
In the Bible, the meaning of the name Alexander is: one who assists men.

A King, a Defender and an Assister. A curious evaluation on what happens when we name people, because these are all meanings that could be ascribed to my character. A consistent narrative around Black men is to consider ourselves as king, as a means of retaining our own importance in the world above the rest. Spiritual leaders and emperors have been named Alexander in history.

In the Bible, Alexander was in the Book of Timothy. A heretic. A man who, alongside Hymenaeus, taught what is believed to be antinomianism within Christianity, which takes the principle of salvation by faith and divine grace to the point of asserting that the saved are not bound to follow the moral law contained in the Ten Commandments.

This distinction between antinomian and other Christian views on moral law is that antinomians believe that obedience to the law is motivated by an internal principle flowing from belief rather than from any external compulsion. It grows clearer and clearer to me that my parents didn't have a clue of the burden they were giving me when they named me. A heretic, with a name fit for a king or pope. Maybe they did.

Our names are assigned to us at birth until death and have an influence on what I call our cultural compass: the driving force for how we navigate our cultural and personal identities.

Having grown up in the United Kingdom as a British-born West Indian man, I am convinced my place in the world is unique. The very fact that my name wasn't in fact a *typical* West Indian one, along the lines of Arthur, Winston, Everton or even Clarenceford, led me to question whether my own cultural compass was influenced by the isolated position of people of

West Indian heritage because, for the most part, their iden-tity chiefly relies upon and is influenced by colonial history. Names stripped away from ancestors and thus foreign nominals enforced by slave masters later became a sense of pride by which the 'Europeanness' of a name was placed above the rest. The loftier the better. It seems that Caribbean parents tend to free themselves up to names of grand importance for their children. Whether it be an idol or a name they will feel proud to call, or imagine it would look good on a CV. They can choose any name for their children.

As our African heritage was altered by the legacy of slavery and colonialism, language and spiritual practice were both impacted, influencing what we call ourselves. As you can see, it is complex.

First, though, the fact my name is unequivocally English, for a time in my childhood led me to view myself in terms of whiteness and Englishness. Alexander wasn't one of the typical older-fashioned names that are usually given to Caribbean men, such as the aforementioned, but it has been proven to stand the test of time.

Yet, growing up, I didn't really feel that my name connected to me to my culture. The name had no relation to my Caribbean heritage – but it is my father's middle name. It had nothing to do directly with Jamaica, but everything to do with my family.

Catching up on an episode of the ABC award-winning dramedy *Black-ish* over a weekend struck me as a sign I should write this. Season three, episode fourteen was interesting in that it explored the dynamics of what bearing a name has on a child. The Johnsons were having their fifth. The gender-reveal party burst the balloon and showed it was going to be a boy, the third male addition to the cohort.

What interested me was that patriarch Dre, played by Anthony Anderson, wanted to name the boy Devante, which raised some interesting questions about the naming of a Black child in the

West. His argument was that he had named all of his other children racially ambiguous names, Zoe, Andre Jr, Jack and Diane, and wanted to give his last child a name that he liked, as well as being an obvious statement of their Blackness.

His wife, played by Tracee Ellis Ross, said that she wanted a more conventional name (ironic since her name is Rainbow in the show).

This could most definitely be read as concern for their child's future, but also makes it clear about what Rainbow has been taught to think about the way Black people have to experience the West, when their culture actively works against them. Her upbringing was unconventional. Mixed race, with a carefree mother and father, who were feminist and sex-positive with casual nudist tendencies. Dre, as he comically reiterates every episode, was a product of the 'hood'. While the couple come to an agreement on the name, the initial battle for respectability or palatable names spearheads an interesting question about the intention of name choice. Would they rather life be easier for their child in the future by giving them a name that has no face? Or does the meaning and intention behind it surpass it all?

This was also highlighted in Angie Thomas's award-winning novel, *The Hate You Give*, which has a huge emphasis on names. The main character, Starr, is caught in the middle of the Black Lives Matter campaign, but the names of the young Black people in the story were intentionally placed to overthrow the Eurocentric connotations of what makes a name acceptable.

In the movie adaptation, there is a scene where Starr's father is accosted by the police in front of his family and aggressively searched. He takes them home and, riled up by the way he was assaulted in front of his family, he lines his children, eldest son Seven, Starr and youngest son Sekani, up in the front yard and makes them remember why he chose those names for them all.

Seven was because it was the perfect number. Sekani means 'joy' in a number of African languages, while Starr: 'I look at the stars again. Daddy says he named me Starr because I was his light in the darkness. I need some light in my own darkness right about now.'

She goes on to lead a protest and be a witness in the case that saw her friend, Khalil, killed for reaching for a hairbrush. Khalil is an Arabic name meaning 'good friend'.

Does my name have any dignity in comparison to my African friends?

I don't wish to be tactless, but there is something to be said about Kunta Kinte's ordeal in Alex Haley's *Roots*. (Another Alex. Another timeless story.)

A thirteen-year-old me sat down in front of the television with my siblings, watching, horrified, Kunta being whipped into submission as he was renamed 'Toby'. He lost his religion and his freedom along with his name.

I have many African friends who have varying reactions to their own given names. From West to East. Well known, to lesser known. All expressing different cultures, values and language. Increasingly, many are opting to choose Christian/Western names in order to, in my observation, have some semblance of ease within the culture. Growing up, this was most certainly the case. While the cultural shift is changing and more and more West Africans are embracing their African cultural names, it is quite telling that in order to survive in this society we have to conform to it. Literal survival in the workplace and school means the acceptance and watering down of cultural identity, thus throwing the compass off.

Language importance comes into play here, as this element supersedes my Caribbean-ness. It is the driving force and power behind names. For example, I have never seen a Creole name. Our names are rooted in colonialism. Yoruba and Igbo names for example are literal blessings and wishes. Ghanaian names are attributed to the day of the week, with deeper elemental meanings.

As a person of West Indian descent, names are grounded in Christianity, since it was the predominant culture, or – not uncommon in most cultures – the memory of another person. These bind us to our heritage, but because the heritage is steeped in the colonial mindset, I feel the cultural gap widens.

Once, I sat down with my mother and asked her what my name meant and why she and my father had decided to choose the name. She told me that she didn't know what it meant at the time, but she had always liked the name Alexander and thought it would be fitting for her son.

It helps that it is my father's middle name, but other than that, my name doesn't seem to explicitly fit into any aspect of my Black life here in Britain. When I went to school, university and even work, my name was an 'easy' one to remember. A commonplace proper noun that has been used by so many for so long, it has long lost its uniqueness.

In an old workplace of mine, there were four Alexs, three Toms and several Sams. There seems to be an instrumental factor in English, and possibly Western European culture, that has a sort of flippancy when picking names for children. To say there are days where I wish I could have just walked into predominantly white spaces and professed a name that they struggled to pronounce and that held weight to my own cultural identity and compass is an understatement.

In the answer to the question 'what is your name?', there was a period where I thought of answering 'Kwesi', which would give me some kind of shimmer. 'Black magic'. I decided against it. I thought it would be appropriation-adjacent, but I was born on a Sunday. When I look at a Ghanaian man who was born on the same day, and see that they have a specific name that pertains to that day, it is Kwesi.

To rally back around to the question of uniqueness, when I was younger my cousin Dionne and I were talking about names on a keyring and how her name was always misspelt. In typical childish mockery where I jibed that I could never have that problem, she said, 'Well, your name just isn't unique, Alex. Everyone has it. Boys and girls.'

Being Black and British is both a conundrum and a grey area, filled with respectability, politics and performance. You can't wear the culture that you come from because it is seen as primitive and alien in a way that promotes shame and embarrassment, even mockery, from both inside and outside of the community. Culture – the hair we hide, the clothes we wear, the music we listen to, the food we eat and the way we speak – has to be tapered and minimised in white spaces, and our names don't evade this either.

We don't have to look too far in history to see Caribbeans and Africans mocking one another in the UK, one culture trying to get the upper hand while battling against the explicit racism of whites in this country, all aspiring to some form of acceptance in this quite oppressive country.

However, following generations formed a culture that explored and expressed identity here, still trying to hold on to whatever it meant to be Black (your immediate culture behind closed doors) and British (the culture you were confronted with outside of your home).

By accepting Black Britishness, are we expected to lose our inherent cultural identities? More and more children of African descent can't speak their mother tongue. More and more Caribbean people born in the UK have never been to the Caribbean, creating wider cultural distances with back home.

With prevailing economic and psychological constraints and the need to 'belong' by parents, there's a disadvantage in wanting to be accepted in a society that finds it difficult to accept you as you are.

My ancestors, forced to work on Caribbean soil and once transported from Africa, have seen generation after generation of African culture wiped out, to be taken over by Britishness. I maintain that this is a mentality that needs to be broken.

And pop culture supports the performance even more. As much as people embraced the Marvel film *Black Panther* as a box-office hit, and leagues of people are now embracing African images in Hollywood, I am not sure that many understood the impact that names have on the African diaspora, even more importantly, as seen on the big screen. Royal men's names began with the consonant before the apostrophe (T'Chaka, T'Chala, W'Kabi, M'Baku, N'Jobu), while women's names were one uninterrupted word (Nakia, Shuri, Okoye), but non-royal men also shared this attribute (as in the instance of Zuri). The importance of the name came when Erik Killmonger was taken to the throne room. He began to tell the room who he was in English and it wasn't until he was challenged by one of the tribe leaders that he spoke in Xhosa and revealed his name as N'Jadaka, son of N'Jobu, the brother of T'Chaka.

Yes, we saw an amalgamation of continental cultures reflected in the story, as well as the unwavering and unashamed potence of Africanness, but I felt like there was something so important and intentional in the names that *Black Panther* had created to strengthen African identity, albeit from a Central–South African gaze. So much so, we should not be surprised when we see the new generation of children named after Shuri or Nakia. For their qualities (as fictional characters who are scientists, warriors and strong and encouraging women with agency) rather than just the meaning of their names.

Further to this, I have recently read a book called *Children of Blood and Bone* by a Nigerian–American author called Tomi Adeyemi. As well as skilfully investigating racial tensions and persecution through West African fantasy, the importance of names holds strong throughout. West African fantasy notwithstanding, there is yet another subtle importance of *name*. In the book, Zélie, her brother, T'Zain, and a refugee princess, Amari, are on the run; they come into contact with a legendary *sêntaro* (high priest) who could help them restore magic to Orïsha. With the magic in Orïsha gone, Yoruba, the magical language, was banished with it. However, in the scene, Zélie and the party ask him his name, to which he replies, 'Lekan'. And in a moment of intense profundity, she responds, 'Olamilekan . . . *my wealth is increased.*' The moment is made much more poignant when he says, 'You remember your language.' The legacy of the name and the language was making a comeback. Hope was on the fringes of of returning. This was a beautiful way of describing how our heritage, our magic, can be wiped from us. Lekan saying 'you remember your language' is tantamount to 'you remember who you are'.

Respectability politics sees us de-*ethnicise* the names we have. Many of my West African friends have adopted, or were given, Christian names as a way of aiding assimilation. To me, I was none the wiser. I grew up with people like Chris and Charles. I knew Chris was Ghanaian, but he told me his *real* name was Kwame, and Charles's *actual* Yoruba name was Deji – possibly short for Ayodeji (*my joy has become two*) or Oladeji (*my wealth has become two*). Once this was revealed, I felt both somewhat perplexed at the thought that they would hide such strong names, and irritated that they had let us call them what I now deemed as foreign names. I would have had no problem calling 'Charles' Ayo or Deji or 'Chris' Kwame, but in some cases adopting another name might be seen as a self-protective tactic – a 'this is my FAMILY name' utility.

My Nigerian friend's mum got into a conversation about names. As she was Yoruba, we spoke about name mispronunciation and allocation. She told me my name would be 'Abiodun', which means *'born in a festive period'*. This stuck with me because, as previously mentioned, each person's name usually represents a blessing, a position or a special circumstance. This is what you lose when you de-ethnicise. I then thought about my position in the Black British diaspora as a Caribbean man.

In Trevor Noah's book, *Born A Crime,* he speaks about how he was called 'Trevor' and not something explicitly South African in a segment describing the various meanings of relatives' names and the direct parallels with their characters. When it came to him, he said his mother made a calculated choice not to give him a binding name.

He said: 'When it was time to pick my name, she [his mother] chose Trevor, a name with no meaning whatsoever in South Africa, no precedent in my family. It's not even a Biblical name. It's just a name. My mother wanted her child beholden to no fate. She wanted me to be free to go anywhere, do anything, be anyone.'

I agree with this. There is something powerful in not wanting to make your children beholden to any fate, but there is also the power of altered intention, whereby his mother could have named him a Xhosa name that rooted him in South Africa but still gave him a fighting chance globally. Whether it be a middle name or not.

Granted, I have never had my name mispronounced. I have never had my name misappropriated and made into a nickname. To this day, I will never understand why in this British education system, we can say names like Dostoevsky, Beethoven and Tchaikovsky and yet Temilade or Ayobami become the hardest thing for people to accept. Over time, I guess familiarity has stood the test, but we cannot avoid the fact that Eurocentricity self-perceives itself as most important.

On this, my friend's mum said: 'If you call my name wrong, you have dissolved it of its intended meaning. Don't say our names wrong.'

Humanise us. Don't pronounce the name wrongly. Give us the basic human courtesy of getting it right.

In my quest, I found an interest in Arawak and Taíno names.

I began to look around at which names were prevalent in the Caribbean before colonisers ruined the region. It had many different tribes and chiefdoms within it on the island of Hispaniola (Dominican Republic and Haiti). Along the way, I found out about a queen or *cacica* (chief) of Xaragua (now Léogâne, Haiti). The *cacica's* name was Anacaona. 'Ana' means 'flower' and 'caona' means 'gold' or 'golden', which translates her name as the 'Golden Flower'. She was one of the last queens on the island, and was the first to come into contact, alongside her brother, Bohechio, with Christopher Columbus. The devastation and pillaging that occured in the region was a major disgrace in the European colonisation of this planet, and spurred the way for slaves to be brought there from Africa and for capitalism to grow in the West.

In Jamaica, the Taíno cultures continued, but to ensure their survival they intermarried with Maroons (Africans who had escaped from slavery and mixed with the indigenous peoples of the islands), where matrilineal culture continued and was enhanced by the Ghanaian influence, as most were reported to be from Ghana followed by the Bight of Benin, as a consequence of slavery. Taínos had a matrilineal culture. The Maroons in Jamaica were led by a Ghanaian woman called Nanny, and formed their settlements in the mountains, while terrorising slave plantations, hoping to free slaves.

It has therefore been made apparent to me that my culture is a powerful and rich one, so when considering a name for my children, if I endeavour to have any, I would consider looking at Taíno, West African (and *possibly* European) names based upon my heritage.

Children should know who they are, and while, to me, this is what it means to be directly connected to the land and legacy, I think that it is also an important factor when considering the cultural compass of Caribbean children. Are we too accepting as British-born Caribbeans? Do we take what is handed to us in the form of English and Christian names, or names that we like from a myriad of languages that surpass our own?

As well as choosing typically English (or French and Spanish, depending on the culture of consequence) Christian names, I found that many were chosen as namesakes and a love for the way they sound, feel and even look on the page. Aesthetics – some may want French names for all of their children or for them to be named after celebrities. Does that cheapen the way that we experience name ownership? In my opinion, it does. A name is not commonplace. It is your stamp on this world. More importance should be placed on names.

My Granny called her youngest child Paul, not because of the saint, but after Paul McCartney. She had a choice of whether it could have been attributed to a saint or a star, and she chose a star. His name means more to me than it does him – for it to be attributed to a living icon that outlived my own grandmother and is not even related to me irks me.

Two of my cousins have names attributed to singers with name meanings considered after the fact, and I have numerous friends named after football players. The sad thing about this is that there is no real connection to these names, just that these people were labelled with this word, this noun, from birth. A conundrum I have only found in the Caribbean community.

On the surface, I do feel like a Jamaican. I eat, drink and consume Jamaica most days. it's a culture I balance with Black Britishness. I tap in through music, through food, through effervescent and slightly anglicised patois – but I just do not feel it in my name. I place name above all of this because, as mentioned above, it is the one thing that links explicitly to culture in a way that shouldn't need to warrant any more interrogation.

If you meet someone and they say their name is 'Oluwatosin', you automatically link the name to a culture. Same with South and East Asian names. Same with typical African American names that I touched upon earlier, but Caribbean names seem to have slipped through the annals of culture and time.

Every time I go back to Jamaica, I feel at home – until someone asks me a question or asks me my name, and I become 'Inglish'. A foreigner.

The fact that our names aren't so rooted to the land and the culture of Jamaica means that there isn't a connection to my small parish in Trelawny or Clarendon. When I go back to Jamaica, I am a foreigner without a cause. When I remain in the UK, in London, I am a foreigner without a name. In short, this essay is a question of belonging. Where do I belong if my culture is Caribbean, but my name Ancient Greek? It wouldn't be so bad if there were Caribbean names and I wasn't named such because I could feel like I had the option and right to adopt said name. A part of me feels like I have no right to adopt a name of a culture that is not mine.

One thing that comes from the West Indian culture is the freedom to name children however they choose. I was named Alexander after my father's middle name. His first name was passed down for three generations but stopped with him. My middle name, Jermaine, was chosen by my mother because she liked it but is in fact a Latin name for 'brother'. That's as much as I know. So while my name was picked as a consequence of my father's name, and his name was picked as a consequence of my grandad's and so forth, there's an element of consistency there.

As for my sister, I was six or seven when I flicked through the baby book of African names and came across the Swahili name, Kamaria. It means 'beautiful/bright like the moon'. And that, she is.

We have to continue to make intentional efforts to name our children something of value. As Caribbean people, our heritage and culture is a tricky line to follow and make sense of: as I have mentioned above, colonial history has wiped our connection to our land and impregnated us with a heritage of regret that, I believe, can be restructured through the way we introduce our children to the world.

Living in a country as cold and distant as Britain, finding our footing on this island is always going to be challenging. When we feel that we have to hide our names as Africans as a form of respectability politics, we shame ourselves into thinking that our 'English' names hold some kind of importance.

While Caribbean people adopt and adapt names, learning the meanings and intent behind the names should be a paramount part of raising the British-born West Indian child. As a British-born Jamaican, I have access to culture like never before, but the one thing I have taken from trying to understand this question of naming and my place through displacement is that we should look at the intention of why we call a child a name. The family history or legacy which is attached to them as well as to us. Looking at what it means to the parent, but also what it means for the child as they grow into, hopefully, well-meaning human beings.

It took me months to write this essay, and while at the conception I felt that my name had no bearing on my person, I look at it differently now because, while I am a continuation of my father and am bound to him through blood and bone, I am also a continuation of my grandfathers, but a beginning of me.

WHAT'S IN A NAME?

My name is Alexander, and it carries the name of my father. It reflects the choice of my grandmother's love from Westmoreland, and the clarity of my mother's confidence from Leicester. That is what is in a name and this is who I am. I am me, but I carry pieces of history within to make me whole.

Fear of a Black Man
Alex Wheatle

It was Brixton, 1978. I had taken a 109 bus from Brixton Hill to Brixton High Street, en route to my social-services offices on Herne Hill Road, just off Coldharbour Lane. Having recently arrived from a Surrey children's home, I was relatively fresh to the racial dynamics in Brixton. Casually dressed in trainers, jeans, T-shirt, anorak and a beige-coloured cloth cap, I enjoyed the sound of reggae music blaring out from cars, houses and 'Brixton suitcases', as I always did when I was out and about there. Within the fifteen minutes it took me to reach my destination, two white women had crossed the road to avoid me and another had clutched her handbag so tightly to her chest, I'm sure it left an imprint of the maker's brand on her clothing. If I ventured further afield to the leafy avenues of Dulwich or the wide pavements of Putney, there was a more than even chance that someone would alert the police about my presence. For young, Black male Brixtonians, this was a daily occurrence.

It was the same whenever I browsed in shops. The security guard would move stealthily to ensure that he'd always have me or my friends in his vision. He would flex his fingers, shift his eyes and ready himself for a confrontation. The more criminally

minded of my bredrens used this racial profiling to their advantage. They dressed down and entered clothing stores in the West
End. They purposefully acted suspiciously and readily accepted
the unblinkered attention from security while a white accomplice
lifted all manner of garments.

Football hooliganism was at its peak in the late 1970s and
early 1980s. It was a time when shopkeepers located near soccer
grounds would board up their windows on match days. Local
parents instructed their young children to stay indoors. Women
were warned to steer clear of the streets. In a weekly ritual,
rival supporters clashed in pubs, bars and train stations with
crowbars, knuckledusters, bottles and other weapons of choice.
Yet the 'sus law', where the police had the powers to arrest an
individual loitering in a public place if they believed they were
about to commit a crime, was never employed against white
football supporters en route to a football match. In Brixton,
I was once stopped by the police for having an afro comb in
my back pocket. According to the arresting officer, it was an
offensive weapon and I had behaved menacingly. 'What?' I said.
'Are you saying I can't flick out my afro? You gotta be fucking
kidding me!'

Inhabiting a black skin was mistrustful enough for them.

These were the days of police intimidation, beatings in cells
and forced confessions. No statements or witness accounts were
filmed or recorded. I've never heard of an account where a Black
man was assaulted by a single officer while in custody – there
were always three or more assailants. The mere presence of a
Black man, perceived by most of white society as wild, violent
and sexually dangerous, led to a fear that had to be eradicated.

In 1955, it was this same irrational dread coupled with
entrenched racism that led to two white men, Roy Bryant and
J. W. Milam, abducting and mutilating the fourteen-year-old
Black boy, Emmet Till, before shooting him in the head and

dropping his body into the Tallahatchie River, Mississippi. The supposed crime that Emmet Till committed was to flirt with Bryant's white wife, Carolyn.

I have visited Emmet Till's shrine at the National Museum of African American History in Washington DC. I stood perfectly still as I viewed the original casket Emmet's body was buried in. Although Emmet's face was hideously deformed, at his funeral, his mother decided on an open casket so the whole world could witness Emmet's defacement. I couldn't help asking myself, 'What hellish, primal, deep-seated racist fear could cause Bryant and Milam to inflict such appalling injuries on a child?'

A similar fear has led to numerous unarmed Black men being executed by American policemen in more recent times. These same officers never seem to be so anxious or trigger-happy when apprehending white murderers who, in some instances, have slain scores of people. More often than not, they manage to present themselves at court unscarred, unshot and unharmed. Even in extreme cases, the media never labels them terrorists.

Even a silent, still gesture from a Black man can terrify fragile white folks. In London, I was fortunate enough to meet one of my boyhood heroes, Tommie Smith, winner of the 200m sprint at the 1968 Olympic Games in Mexico City. In protest against the way African Americans were dehumanised, killed and condemned to poverty in a rabid, racist society, Tommie Smith and his compatriot, John Carlos, marched out shoeless to their medal ceremony, in black socks and black gloves. As the US national anthem blared out in the huge stadium, the two men raised their black-gloved fists in acknowledgement of those who had fought and lost their lives in the struggle. Mr Avery Brundage, President of the US Olympic Committee, took extreme offence. He immediately suspended Smith and Carlos from the Games and expelled them from the Olympic village. This was the same Avery Brundage who hadn't uttered a murmur of dissent amid the mass Nazi saluting at the 1936 Berlin Games.

Smith and Carlos returned to the US. They struggled financially and initially found it almost impossible to gain meaningful employment. White America has means of making Black men pay for forcing them to face and acknowledge their own atrocities.

Almost half-a-century later, in 2016, the American footballer Colin Kaepernick also discovered that a silent, still gesture, *taking a knee* as the US national anthem was being played before a game, could destroy his job prospects. He was protesting against a country that oppressed Black people and people of colour. He was regarded as one of the best quarterbacks of his generation, and after opting out of his San Francisco 49ers contract, as I write, no National Football League franchise has offered him an opportunity to resurrect his career. Oh yes, they'll always make us pay. Even though Nike, a predominantly white transnational conglomerate, has made Kaepernick the face of their latest advertising campaign, the elite athlete has been denied the right to perform what he does best. Kaepernick's stance has echoes of Muhammad Ali refusing the US army's draft to fight in Vietnam in 1967. They stripped him of his World Heavyweight boxing title and only on appeal was he permitted to fight again in 1970. Ali said at the time, 'No Vietcong ever called me a nigger.'

For the Black man to be fully accepted, we have to strive to be perfect, compliant and not seen as a threat or an uncomfortable reminder of a genocidal colonial past. This can be seen in the 1967 film *Guess Who's Coming to Dinner*, in which Sidney Poitier, the esteemed Black actor, stars alongside Spencer Tracy and Katharine Hepburn. Poitier plays the Black fiancé of a young white woman who is presenting him to her parents for the first time. Poitier's character, Dr John Wayde Prentice Jr, is an impossibly idealistic man who graduated from a top school, began medical initiatives in Africa, is faultlessly groomed and, wait for it, even refused to partake in premarital sex. I love Sidney Poitier, but I detest this movie with a passion because it says to the Black man that for white middle-class society to accept us, we have, in effect, to conduct ourselves like a godly image only found on the ceiling of the Sistine Chapel.

In 1981, in the UK, white alarm reached new heights when Black people held their 'Day of Action' march, protesting against police apathy and inaction following the New Cross Fire, where thirteen young Black youngsters lost their lives. '*Thirteen dead, nothing said,*' we chanted. As we crossed Blackfriars Bridge that day, I witnessed first-hand the growing panic and racial taunts from the police, even though the rally was peaceful. In the present day, I have recognised the same fright in white teachers when Black male students banter or argue boisterously in school classrooms and corridors. They overreact and escalate the tension in a way they would never do if they were addressing white boys. Black male pupils are much more likely to be excluded from schools than their white counterparts for the same offence. Similarly, when Black men enter the justice system, they are more likely to receive longer sentences than white men for identical crimes. On first glance, Black men are perceived as more of a physical threat to society than any other racial group. The statistics don't lie.

As an award-winning writer, even I'm not immune to a mild sense of apprehension when I'm speaking at high-society venues and prestigious book festivals. I arrived at a prominent literary festival wearing casual clothes (as mostly every other author does). As I walked into the Green Room, I sensed suspicious eyes on me, a sudden alertness and stiffening of shoulders. To date, I've been asked if I'm in the band. Do I know where the cloakroom is? Am I aware this is the Green Room and only reserved for writers? Where can I get a drink? This space is not for the public – and my favourite: are you lost? On all of these occasions, I detected a small dose of trepidation at my presence, an over-compensating smile and an obvious relief when I explain that I'm a writer. I try to be as approachable as I possibly can but sometimes the old rebel in me would like to produce my best Brixton scowl.

When I'm going about my daily business, I sense this unease, this fear of a Black man. Simply waiting for my turn at an ATM machine can cause anxious glances over shoulders and a hurried look along the street for potential support. I'm confronted by a similar nervousness when I attempt to gain entry late at night into a club or bar. The eyes betray the bouncers' thoughts – is this Black man here to cause trouble?

I have to peel back the years to try and understand this illogical terror.

Slavemasters excused their abominable behaviour towards their Black captives by convincing themselves and others that their slaves were animals. From South Carolina, John C. Calhoun, the 7th Vice President of the United States, said in a famous 1837 speech defending slavery: 'Never before has the black race of Central Africa, from the dawn of history to the present day, attained a condition so civilised and so improved, not only physically, but morally and intellectually.'

The implication was blatant. According to Calhoun and his fellow slavery apostles, Black people were subhuman. Articles debating the slavery/antislavery issue were published in the *Charleston Mercury*. Numerous slaveholders strongly believed that 'slavery would liberate Africans from their savage-like ways'.

So, my ancestors were granted the status of 'animal'. This rank has seeped into the consciousness of many ignorant white people over many centuries and decades. It's taught to their children and passed on to their children's children. Now, the hatred is whipped out and fanned by right-wing media commentators, politicians and social-media trolls. The 45th President of the United States says they are fine people. It always disturbs me when racists believe they have a licence to brand us as 'monkeys', 'apes' and 'gorillas', anything inhumane and not quite civilised. I switch TV channels when I'm watching a soccer match and I hear monkey chants whenever a Black player nears the ball. For me, the insults dredge up the belief that Black people need 'slavery to liberate Africans from their savage-like ways'.

The racist abuse perpetuates the myth that we are untamed, wild and dangerous. Hence the wary glances, the tightening of shoulders and the mild tension in the cheeks as I enter a Green Room at an esteemed literary festival.

My spirit informs me that Black people carry a sense of injustice in their bloodline (Rastafarian brethren are always instructing me that *the blood remembers*). I also believe that those who have greatly benefited from our slave state have this subconscious and wholly conscious dread that one day there will come a reckoning, when we will exact a merciless revenge. It's why in the past our freedom fighters were quickly silenced and executed.

There are numerous slave revolts I could mention that occurred in Jamaica, but I'll relate the story of 'Tacky', who was born in my mother's parish of St Mary. In 1760, Tacky and his band killed their slave masters and took over a nearby fort that contained guns and ammunition. The British sent in reinforcements. More slaves from adjacent plantations joined the rebellion and the battle raged for a number of days. Tacky was hunted down and finally captured. His severed head was displayed on a long pole in Spanish Town to serve as a warning to others. Rather than return to a slave state, many of Tacky's followers committed suicide in coastal caves. They didn't teach me tales like this when I was at school.

Over a hundred years later, a similar fate awaited another Jamaican freedom fighter, Paul Bogle, and he wasn't even a slave. He was a man of the church, who stood up for the rights of Black people. That didn't save him. He led hundreds of black peasants on a march to the Morant Bay court house protesting against the trial of a Black man who had allegedly trespassed on long abandoned plantation land. The defendant was convicted. Another Black man hollered his disapproval and he was immediately arrested. This act infuriated the crowd. The police were beaten and forced to retreat. Twenty-five people lost their lives in the initial insurrection. Par for the course, the British government sent in reinforcements. They killed four hundred revolutionaries across the parish and Paul Bogle was executed.

If the present monarchy have truly changed and want to be actively seen as representative to all who dwell in the UK, I suggest that on the next visit to Jamaica by someone from the Royal household, they should lay a wreath at Paul Bogle's memorial in Morant Bay and step back respectfully.

'*No chains on my feet but I'm not free*,' Bob Marley and the Wailers sang in the early 1970s. The Jamaican reggae icon never killed anyone but the CIA kept a file on him because they knew he had the rhetoric, the intelligence and the power to rouse the Black masses. To put it simply, they feared him.

To this day, the message to us is clear: if we see you as a threat, if you force us to confront our vile colonial past, if you dare to question our morality, beliefs and self-righteousness, if you light the flame of Black consciousness and solidarity, we will find ways to silence you, discredit you and eliminate the way you make your living. Muhammad Ali and Colin Kaepernick can bear witness to that.

In 2001, I published what I consider my most important novel, *East of Acre Lane*. It's set against the backdrop of the 1981 Brixton uprising and brutal police oppression, acting under what I regarded as an inherently racist Conservative government. It was critically acclaimed wherever it was reviewed. If I can indulge in a little head-swell for a moment, here are quotes from three of them:

> 'Treading a Dubliners-esque terrain which swallows up the Brixton landscape, the novel spits out the simmering frustrations of being young, Black and British during the Thatcher years ... Wheatle retells a shaping episode in recent British history and tellingly captures as much of today's mood as he does of an unforgettable 1981'
> Pride Magazine

> 'A vibrant and highly evocative insight into one of the most explosive periods in London's history'
> Scotland on Sunday

> 'Wheatle has written a hard-hitting novel which is an incendiary reminder of one of the most explosive events in London's post-war history'
> Big Issue

After assessing my reviews, please forgive me if I expected to be feted at literary festivals, named on shortlists for book prizes, my text to be included as essential reading on the national curriculum and serialisation rights on BBC radio. Yes, I did dream. For a year or two, the book was even optioned by the BBC as a potential drama for television. I went to my bed in those days thinking good things. Gosh, how naïve was I.

None of the above happened.

I believe I was seen as a threat, a Black man who made white people feel uncomfortable by my presence and the words I put on the page. *East of Acre Lane* was too incendiary. Amid descriptions of vivid racial violence, it contained depictions of a young Black male wanting to kill police officers. I guess I didn't quite tick the boxes like Poitier's Dr John Wayde Prentice Jr. I didn't graduate from a top school, attend Oxbridge or any other top-ranking university. Alex Wheatle's an angry, uneducated Black man from Brixton who was raised in a children's home. What true artistic merit can flow from his unschooled pen? It's better to promote Black narrative texts that are palatable to sensitive white tongues.

If we can push my novel aside for a moment and consider this: why hasn't one of the most significant events in Black British history ever been dramatised for UK terrestrial television?

Since the publication of *East of Acre Lane,* it's only through sheer persistence, fierce stubbornness and what talent I possess that I have managed to fashion a career in this old writing game, for so long the domain of white middle-class men. I'm still driven by this overriding urge to write *our* narrative.

I yearn for the day when I can walk into an establishment, wearing my casual clothes, my red, gold and green shoulder bag, listening to Dennis Brown on my headphones, and not be given a flicker of attention or perceived as the slightest of threats. I don't think that day will come in my lifetime.

For the unaccountable atrocities that my ancestors had to endure, it is me who should cower in the presence of white men. It is me who should look up and down the street for potential support in case of an unprovoked assault and me who should be mistrustful of a paler skin. But it is me who is still seen as a menace to society.

And Me . . .

Courttia Newland

I'm going to talk about something that I've largely kept to myself. It's odd, as I consider myself a writer of extreme honesty that I try to carry over into real life, and yet even now I'm hesitating, and I realise to some degree I've procrastinated even more than usual about the thinking, and writing of this. The committing of a hidden life event to the posterity of the written word. That's always a scary act. I used to wonder if my reluctance was driven by shame, or simply my incredulity at the nature of what took place all those years ago. Now I think that it is those things mostly, but also a hell of a lot more. Over the last few years, particularly in the recent crosswinds of our racial and cultural political climate, this life event bubbled to the surface of my memory, never quite boiling over. I've talked about it to a few of my close male friends, that's it. And I almost never mention it to women.

So OK. I'll stop stalling and try to be as straightforward as I can.

A few decades ago, when I was just becoming a published author, I was discussing projects with various companies. In one, I dealt with a white male creative, and when he left I was assigned to someone else, a white woman. I was overjoyed to be taken seriously at last, a bit starry-eyed from the blitz of media and publishing parties, both of which I was unused to. My new contact, charming and jovial, was full of great ideas and encouragement. We hit it off and got to work right away.

I'd travel into their offices a few days a week, full of excitement. I was in my early twenties, eager to change the world. We'd sit in a room together and thrash out story outlines. Almost right away, my editor began making personal comments that I found highly unprofessional. She had black women friends, she said, who would 'love me.' She said I was cute, and sometimes when we were sitting at a desk side by side, she'd stare into my face when we were meant to be working. It was very unnerving, and while I appreciated the compliments, which would occur every time we worked together, I began to feel a little uncomfortable in her presence. Not long afterwards, she suffered a small injury. There was a meeting due, and she called me up, insisting that I came to her house. Given what had been going on in the office I wasn't that keen, so I asked if we could meet in a public place. She refused. We went back and forth until the conversation ended with her screaming down the phone, swearing at me, and insisting I came to her house. I refused. The following day, someone in the company rang me up to inform me I had lost the job.

I tried to fight it, but there was nothing I could do. The whole deal collapsed. I knew what had happened to me was a commonplace occurrence for women, and I'd long felt outraged about that reality, but I quickly saw there was no outrage for me. When I spoke to anyone about what happened, there was a sympathetic shrug, and a change of subject. I responded the same way the majority of people would in this situation. I let it go.

It's clear to me that this incident is an example of white female privilege being used to dominate a young black man. I was perceived to have no recourse, no agency. I had to submit to being exoticised, and when I refused to reciprocate I was punished. It wasn't the first time I'd seen this happen, and it wouldn't be the last opportunity I would lose because of something said about me by a white woman. Yet I'd never seen that privilege levelled at me in such a negative manner until that first loss. It was shocking, and frightening to think of my intended reality from outside perspectives. My most recent loss was a university teaching post. Only the interventions of other students saved my professional reputation, but the ultimate fallout was that I lost the job anyway.

Many years after, as the fallout from Harvey Weinstein's crimes rippled and spread, and the #MeToo movement rose in its wake, I was reminded of my first experience in the media, of negative experiences involving white women from childhood to present day, of events that happened to friends, or have occurred within the wider diasporic Black community. And although it's obvious that none of my personal experiences come anywhere close to the heinous crimes of rape and enforced sexual harassment committed globally by men, I have seen white privilege used by women as an oppressive tool far too many times to believe there should not be the same level of accountability.

I'll hold my hands up right now and admit this is a complicated thing to tackle. I know this, which has in part fuelled my hesitance to bring up the subject. So while I fully support any movement that seeks to address the rampant misogyny and patriarchy driving our society, and of course includes men of colour on too many occasions, I wonder if it's possible to have a conversation about the role white women play in the continuous oppression of Black men? To speak about this in a historical context, tracing the direct line from enslavement and colonisation to the present day? To have an honest discussion about the fact that white women, who obviously face a cis white male patriarchal system of oppression, also use that patriarchal system to oppress those perceived as lower on the racial and social hierarchy?

I believe we must.

Of course, I'm not writing to generalise a whole race and gender. Many white women *do not* use their privilege adversely. Many are allies, instrumental in standing beside us, even speaking on subjects such as this. They exist. We see them and acknowledge their presence. The fact that they benefit from a system designed to work better for them than those designated 'beneath them' does not mean some do not fight for social and political improvement on our behalf. That much should be obvious, although I feel it must be stated here to avoid the very real chance of being misconstrued.

Still, the fact remains that the Black man's very complicated relationship with white women is fraught with a complexity rarely addressed, alongside how it bleeds into white women's complicated relationship with the supremacist patriarchy that in turn oppresses them. Oftentimes, this conversation is framed as an examination into the lengths Black men go to mine sexual otherness, or exoticism – Black men's appreciation sex clubs almost exclusively peopled by white women, mock plantation orgies, Beach Boy holidays in Africa and the Caribbean. These examinations are usually from a feminine perspective. What's missing is any deep analysis of Black male psychology. The mental displacement needed to attend those parties and become a 'bull' for the night, or be paraded on the arm of a white woman in Hasting, Barbados. Is prostitution less morally demeaning if a man is the prostitute, a woman the client? Why is this seen as less mentally destructive, or nuanced?

Not having lived any of those experiences, I'm unable to speak with confidence on either, but I do think closer dissection is more than necessary. For myself and many others, our exoticisation and real-life negative experiences leads to something less akin to fascination with the white female, and closer to wariness, sometimes outright fear. As Chris Rock would put it, the 'fucking around with white girls' syndrome. We've been bitten too many times; we're thrice shy, perhaps more. Fucking around with white girls, to restate Rock's point all too crassly, is a dangerous pursuit for black men, historically and in present times.

All too often, Black men are scarred by childhood experience. When I was little more than a year old my parents moved to the west London suburbs of Uxbridge, Middlesex. We were one of only three Black families. It was there that a reception schoolteacher insisted I draw my mother pink rather than brown, forcing me to tears. I was three. Years later, a woman racially abused and fought my mother outside those same primary-school gates. Of course, my mother gave as good as she got. We left Uxbridge when I was eight, after my parents' separation and settled back into zone two, west London. There was no way my mother was going to live in Uxbridge and raise two Black boys by herself.

I was already reading heavily. As a teenager, my mother bought me Ntozake Shange's *Betsey Brown*. I loved it. On page ninety-six I encountered a hazy ancestor veiled in mystery. 'Emmett Till was my age, Aunt Jane,' a boy named Charlie said. On the next page, Charlie told his younger male cousin, 'We gonna get some white tail and say we did it for Emmet Till.'

I was Till's age too.

A visitation, a haunting. The name lodged in my mind and remained. This was the 1980s. I had no idea who Charlie was talking about. Research in those pre-internet days was largely inadvertent. I read more books, which led me to others, and eventually discovered the story of Emmet Till, the Chicago boy who went South to visit relatives in Money, Mississippi. There, he entered a grocery store where he was accused of flirting, touching the hand, and wolf whistling at Carolyn Byrant, the store cashier. Four days later, on 28 August 1955, Roy Bryant, Carolyn's husband, and his half-brother J. W. Milam kidnapped Till, beat him, dragged him to a river bank, shot him, tied him to a seventy-four-pound gin fan with barbed wire and shoved his corpse into the river.

Till's mother Maime opted for an open-casket funeral. In her own words, it was to 'let the world see what has happened, because there is no way I could describe this. And I needed somebody to help me tell what it was like.' Because of her strength and courage, some ten thousand people saw her son's body, Revd Jesse Jackson claimed. It went on to become the largest civil-rights demonstration in civil history.

A truth telling, a whisper. In 2008, some fifty-three years later, Carolyn Bryant gave an interview to Timothy B. Tyson, an author and a senior research scholar at Duke University, in which she told him she'd lied under oath on the witness stand. Till never grabbed her waist and uttered obscenities. 'That part is not true,' she told Tyson. To this day, it's unclear whether any part of the alleged flirtation between Till and Bryant actually took place, but as she knows and admits, 'Nothing that boy did could ever justify what happened to him.'

Till's death serves as a marker in American history and their Civil Rights movement, but it also a mark of how dangerous contact between Black men and white women has been for both since the days of mass African enslavement. It's no surprise to see how such brittle contact has become fetishized, held up as an advancement of both freedom and Black male success, however misguided those ideologies may be. Three years after the murder, thousands of miles across the Atlantic, there came an assault on Majbritt Morrison, a white Swedish women, by a group of white youths made aware that she was married to Raymond Morrison, a West Indian. The youths threw milk bottles at Morrison, calling her 'Black man's trollop', and reputedly struck her on the back with an iron bar. The resulting hostilities, which included attacks on West Indian houses and involved over 300 white people over five days, became known as the Notting Hill race riots. When the violence subsided, there was a concerted effort to heal previous rifts. A precursor to the present-day Notting Hill Carnival was organised by the activist Claudia Jones in 1959, held in St Pancras Town Hall. Interracial relationships of all kinds, particularly between Black men and white women, became less fraught with danger: although old prejudices and former concerns never quite diminished.

And on and on, until the present day. While it's true that white-supremacist belief has been imbibed by a certain number of Black men, causing them to accept the lie of white women's superiority above all others, it's also true that all too often Black men are the subject of their racist ire. Social media's a slippery ally, on occasion doing as much to hinder as help the cause of social justice, but it's been exemplary at charting the numerous cases of white women caught in 'acts of oppression'. These can have as humble catalysts apartment manager Erica Walker's insistence that a black man shouldn't wear socks by the pool (she called the police when he refused to leave), or the woman who rang 911 on a group of Black people barbecuing in an Oakland park. White women have called the police on Black men 'loitering' in Starbucks while waiting for a friend, a Black girl selling water in San Francisco, and even most recently a Black woman sheltering from the rain.

What's shocking for those who've never seen this level of unchecked discriminatory aggression is the rampant privilege behind their attempts to weaponize protectors of the civilian population as racist tools. They believe the police will act in their service because they perceive this is what the police do. It's something Black people have been saying since for ever, and has become even more menacing in the Trump era. Now most people have a video-recording facility on their phones, it's something millions get to *see*. I wonder how many people have been arrested, jailed or killed in unseen violent confrontations.

No one wants to be shot for trying to take a business meeting, but the possibility rears its grim head again, and again, and again.

Although it's not particularly analytical, I find it interesting to make a return to social media and view the online response when Black men raise this topic, or even when they don't. I've routinely seen posts where Black men are accused of having very little to complain about, other than whether white women 'like us'; that, if a little thing such as our likeability and racism in general were cleared up, Black men would declare the problem solved. It's also disappointing that most of the time these declarations are written, and intensely felt by Black women. It seems an odd conflict; on the one hand social media proves that contact with certain types of white women can ruin your day, if not your life. On the other lies the argument that all Black men have to fear is whether we're deemed sexually viable by said women. The two viewpoints are far from compatible, and shows that greater dialogue between a diverse range of Black people is vital, where all sides of the argument are heard. Our problems seem less about any particular gender's predisposition to inter-racial relationships, to pick one example, and more about how white-supremacist thought affects society as a whole, normal-ising modes of behaviour that permeate every facet of the way we experience the world, at any moment of our lives.

All I can articulate at this point in time, as a solo writer putting one word after another, is a feeling, which I'm quick to add doesn't belong to Black men alone. Many in the African diaspora recognise it. That feeling is one of intense isolation, vulner-ability, the wariness that comes from needing to trust in order to continue with our lives, yet having that trust broken time and again. The fear of being in close proximity with people who might become colleagues, family, lovers, or assailants, accusers, abusers, harassers. The danger of loving someone who might possibly call you a nigger or a Black bastard in the furious heat of a domestic argument. The confusing seesaw desire of wanting to be an ally for someone's struggle while not having your struggle recognised in return.

Amongst my lived experiences I've had white women punch me for getting on the bus before them, say that I'm not good-looking enough to be a successful writer, rub against me on a packed tube train as if I wasn't even there, and as I've said above, be instrumental in me losing two jobs that I know of, possibly more that I don't. After that second incident, I was left in free fall, jobless with a child to raise and a mortgage to pay. Being liked wasn't the issue; my survival was. Something – dumb luck or the spirits of my long-deceased grandmothers – came through for me. I prefer to believe the latter. Throughout it all, and every incident before or since, I've tried to walk as good as I can muster, and live. That's all any Black man wants really, to walk in a straight line and to live. Maybe one day we will.

Treddin' on Thin Ice

Jesse Bernard

I'm the cracks in my skin
Where words were slung, bottles smashed and fists crunch
Somewhere between 'fam don't try me' and
'Babe just a little higher' I find myself again
There I see the ugliness, everything I tried to hide
But the mirror knows all my secrets.
The mirror sees more than the cracks in the skin
But the vessel that carries the dreams of a nigga just trying to find
someone to share the light with.
But the mirror knows all my secrets
And I'm tired of its lies.

Early on, at least in some years gone by, I came to a realisation: every man has a history of violence, whether done unto them or others. With the latter often being a symptom of the former.

It was December 2005. Swiss's 'Cry' was in heavy rotation. The year I got suspended from school. I remember the turn of events that led to that decision by those who had a stake in my education – but failed to invest in my future. We'll get to that in a moment. Suspension from school carries with it a lot of the same stigma that comes with an arrest and ending up in prison. There's the shame that you're demanded to feel by your teachers and parents, but the stripes you earn from your peers means something, well at least it did back then. I spent a week at home from school dealing with the remnants of the wrath my mum had unleashed the weekend before.

Attending a boys' school is one of those experiences that shapes you, but as I came to learn, it's not the best thing. *I suppose* I was wrong for antagonising and essentially offering the guy out, who was also in the year above, but then I think about the power that I held in that situation. Or lack of, depending on your perspective. Arriving at the rear school gates at 12:45, hyped up with Jay Z's 'PSA' replaying, over and over, in my head – it had been released a year or so earlier – and there stood a swarm of spectators already awaiting my entrance.

And there he stood, my opponent who, apart from his name, I knew little about, other than that his defeat would be my acceptance. Ten seconds. That's all it took, a series of punch combos to decide my victory and my prize – a week-long detention and a caution from the police. Victory for what and for whom? Afterwards I was only angry with any and everything around me (see GIF of Idris Elba flipping table in *Luther.*)

In the next few months, trouble found me, even if I avoided it. I'd painted an invisible target on my back that only the teachers could see. And at the time, I'd much rather have had von Strucker as a deputy head than the one I had. One time, he suspended me because he wanted to make an example due to all the media hysteria about knife crime – this was in 2006. Even if it was a Stanley knife I had found in the playground, there was no talking my way out of it; I hadn't developed enough of a slick mouth by this point. This wasn't one of those moments. By this point, my truth had become lies to people who couldn't look beyond the headlines of 2008. The history of violence followed me long after the first suspension – like Hydra, cut one head off, two more take its place, right?

It wasn't my first; living in close proximity to the white working-class sometimes gets you called a 'nigger' every now and then. In the UK, Mark Duggan knew a history of violence, as did Damilola Taylor, Anthony Walker and countless others. I knew after that fight, people like me weren't protected by the institution. I fought and remained steadfast in my truth. I was an example, I knew that, otherwise I would have been in handcuffs instead. It was a 3 on the Fujita tornado scale, with the potential of it reaching 4, and I was aware from a young age that my life depended on my calmness.

Where did my history of violence originate? Who planted the seeds that would lead me to use my fists as the question, and others' faces as the answer? I was raised in a home where words were thrown and skin was broken, only to be put back together by the very hands that caused it, in the name of discipline. But somewhere in all of that, we seek spaces where violence doesn't meet us. So I found sanctuary in an environment I knew full well didn't have enough space for me – unless it was in the detention room. My first fight was in Year 6 of primary school with a kid who had developed the language to call me a nigger. This was 90s working-class Britain: the *hard* racism jumped out. It had taken a while for the other boys to accept him, myself included; he'd joined the school the previous year and many of our friendship circles existed by Year 2. Without full knowledge or context, I reacted the only way I knew how and that was by lashing out. Apples and pears, all things considered really.

It's easy to see where I've ended up in life, at twenty-eight, as fate or a culmination of events that led to this moment. Being Black in Britain, with what they'd call behavioural issues, means that whether at five, fifteen or thirty years old, I'd experience the reality of being seen as aggressive and volatile. I'm more aware of how that perception can lead to a pattern of cataclysmic events. My suspension affected the level of engagement I received from teachers. By sixth form, I was left aside, resulting in A Level results day feeling like the precise moment the Warriors gave up a 3–1 lead in the NBA Finals. I know that because we live it every day. Then I discovered mixed martial arts, or MMA. Traditional Jiu-Jitsu helped me learn the basic principles of discipline between the ages of ten and sixteen, but for the most part it did little to keep me composed in high-tension situations. It's difficult to employ restraint and a measured approach at such a young age, with fleeting emotions. Even more so, in a world where we're told to control anger and rage. But in hostile spaces, violence waits there for your arrival.

But I found my release when I started MMA in my early twenties (this was a mere development from me starting Jiu-Jitsu after watching *Enter The Dragon*), I saw a change in my health and state of mind. Seeing your parents as full, imperfect – and you know what? – fucking messy people, I can't be mad for ever. While paying bills, my parents were getting up at godforsaken hours, being Black, having to be parents somewhere among all that, dealing with bullshit at work and then having to raise me? The spawn of Satan. Spotting that enthusiasm and watering it by taking your child to lessons every Monday evening, after a day of passive aggressiveness from an underachieving manager, is nothing short of magic. If you're working class, those moments *often* are. The kid in me felt like Bruce Banner, who grew in power when provoked, and hit: taking one felt as good as dishing one out. Like when Kano stopped playing football and picked up a mic for the first time.

The reality was that I was caught in a chasm of whiteness – not quite the *sunken place* – but to be myself, I had to fight. Classrooms were the battlefield, teachers were the opposing force; only to go home, wake up and repeat. I got it wrong at times but it taught me valuable lessons about respectability politics and I was sixteen when I consciously stopped subscribing. But as I approach thirty, I've learned that all I can do is find a safe pocket – a quiet place – in this vast, decrepit and washed-up empire that still thinks it's modern modernity. And for me, that's where joy can be found, if only for a minute.

Told to control our anger, the most fiery emotion, yet throughout my life, I was seldom given practical tools on how to keep it at bay. Many of the emotions we have and display have been affected by the white capitalist patriarchal systems we live under and every day we find ways to express them through these lenses. We find them in sports, music, the barbershop and other pastimes and rituals that stave away the daily pressure of existing.

So what would happen if I threw myself into a world of violence where it was controlled and rules were enforced, while still obtaining personal glory? I'd begin to find ways to live with my anger and tame it when necessary. And it doesn't get any easier walking away from confrontations knowing you have the ability to hospitalise someone. The other side to that unlucky coin is that hypermasculinity seeks out challenges and invites it also. There's a perverse behaviour whiteness often displays in which it provokes the anger within Black people, in order to prove we are what they think we are – thugs.

At university, it was no different, particularly with other Black men. It's often joked about how people leave the ends to go to university to become tough and reinvent themselves, however it's quite the contrary. People carry baggage and trauma with them. For many, who came from areas where they saw a stabbing nearly every day, how do we navigate a completely new environment without being given the tools of recovery and healing? Let's not forget, many of us are the children of people who experienced the violence of the National Front only decades ago.

There are few spaces which provide us with an environment free of violence of some kind, especially out here in Babylon (United Kingdom of Great Britain and all its minions). You ever had to call someone out at work for saying the word 'nigger'? That's an otherworldly type of violence that no one trains you for. You end up feeling like Earn in the parking lot in the pilot episode of *Atlanta*. I mean, you could punch your way through it, but that'd create more problems than solve, particularly in a working environment full of white people. Or you face a John Terry-type moment, played off as banter, but what's worse is that there's no protocol for really addressing racism at work. HR departments are about as useful as Derrick Rose in the post-season when it comes to dealing with that kind of stuff. Colin Kaepernick's fight against the NFL (since 2016; it's still ongoing) completely throws the 'diversity' playbook out of the window. Hiring more Black faces may mean the canteen will serve a version of jerk chicken and rice on Tuesdays but, in reality, all we want is just to eat in peace and not be asked passive aggressive questions about 'interesting' smells.

Ultimately, it's about control. The ability to have control over your impulses, actions and consequences. But it also means submitting to them and understanding that on some occasions, the moment is all a part of accepting the decisions made, whether they be mistakes or triumphs. You're faced with the dichotomy of standing your ground, deciding that in situations where sometimes fighting is the only option and walking away. A history of violence as a Black man can mean that any physical confrontation could land us in prison or worse: these days there's little difference. Assimilation can't save you. Our parents could only dream.

The extremities of these factors in my life have led to me being suspended from school twice and arrested, on both occasions for fighting. Blend the ADHD with a quart of hypermasculinity and a dash of internalised anti-Blackness, and life becomes a fantastic display of calamity and stupid decisions. Much like a tornado, offering little to no foresight, at any moment a storm can erupt. Last time I had an F5 on the Fujita scale, I was at the mercy of institutions I had no sway over, and the anxiety, depression and PTSD brought on by an arrest had caused the ADHD to amplify at the age of nineteen, while I spiralled. University brought little escape from violence, not in a town like Hull, which was white working class, with a significant part of the population living below the poverty line. And I'm sure being bottled in the toilets of a pub for expressing my Africanness didn't help that avoidance of violence. In those moments, I felt vindicated in the way I reacted – *man's no dickhead* – and either way they look at it, they still see me as violent.

Delving deep and time travelling are nauseous journeys often filled with guilt and regret. But regret can become an empowering truth. I am a man with a history of violence, that is my crucible, and one that I must bear as I navigate this world. Escaping this truth does little for my development and growth, as I seek to rid myself of the stressors that push me to react in ways that can't be explained except that I am my parents' son. I can't hold it against my second-gen parents any longer. They saw violence as they grew up; they learned as quickly as they learned their ABCs. It was inevitable that I would, too. It's no surprise that we have difficulty maintaining relationships in our twenties; we weren't provided with the tools to know how to. We are like a bunch of Peter Parkers in *Spider-Man* – or Miles Morales – trying to make sense of it all. That's the melancholy in it all, most Black men are trying to Harlem shake through the pressure. But if we shake too much, we may create aftershocks around us.

It's ironic that in order to control the rage that I'm still learning day by day to quell, it can be soothed by throwing myself into a world of competitive violence. Ben Parker's famous words of wisdom – *with great power comes responsibility* – weren't something for Peter to live by, but for all men with some sort of power, particularly those who struggle with internal battles. And for me, that always meant accountability. A history of violence requires that you can otherwise go throughout life unchecked – and that's more dangerous than anything.

I guess as long as we exist in this universe, on this continuum, violence is something we can't avoid and no matter what, we'll always find it lurking in the corners. After all, the violence that men do is felt by others more vulnerable around us, they understand more than we do but to us it's 'not all men'. Especially when you look at all the different ways in which we can inflict upon others, often emotional and sexual. You only have to listen to rap to get a sense of how we treat women around us and it's been normalised in the way we deified the Bill Cosbys, R. Kellys, Nasir Joneses and Kobe Bryants.

We can only acknowledge that violence isn't our history but our present and hold ourselves accountable because of it. Much easier said than done but it's a matter of urgency. Even if we claim that we don't have a history of violence, we can't deny that we've witnessed it in our homes before we saw it in the world. Okonkwo had to know that violence would be his demise; he may not have known the way in which it occurred, but the life he lived knew little peace. And the importance of Chinua Achebe writing that story was to remind us that the trauma of generations past can manage to affect family lines decades later. The Christian missionaries being the sentinels in this story.

The chasm of violence we exist in is in our homes, work environments, school, the outside world, and more sobering is that a lot of it is also within ourselves. We can only seek spaces where it doesn't meet us when we arrive – nor stalk us. Without also seeking out what causes us to respond and react in ways that harm ourselves and others, it's difficult to find a calm tide in the ocean. There was no way The Punisher, Frank Castle, was going to find healing going about things in the way that he did, but men of violence often find short-term reprieve from what haunts them. It's comfortable after all and doesn't need too much introspection. We can't do it alone either.

Luke Cage found healing and recovery in a barbershop and there is something particularly special about the warm presence and atmosphere they can often conjure. Barbershops provide comfort, freedom, brotherhood, companionship, mentorship and sometimes a good laugh. It's the centre of the Black community for men – maybe not for all of us, particularly as they can be heavily heteronormative and masculine – but in a world where violence is around every corner, that retreat can be the remedy to someone's loneliness. No matter where you go, and I've found myself in barbershops all over the diaspora, you walk in, familiarise yourself with the surroundings and before long, you know that this is where you belong. Barbershops are like S.H.I.E.L.D. safehouses in a world run by HYDRA. They're not perfect, nor can you live in them, but for an hour out of your day, it can feel like time drifts without wonder. Find your barbershop, your safe space, wherever that may be.

There's an unceasing quest for peace that I have rarely seen fulfilled in Black people, our environments within the diaspora haven't allowed for it. But where joy embraces us and invites us in, those are the moments where my own history of violence becomes something to overcome and heal from – rather than bathing in it.

Treddin' on thin ice becomes a survival skill after a while, one that allows you to eventually skate through life's woes with finesse and pain. As I've got older, I've realised I don't have to skate if I really don't want to, and for many layered reasons, I shouldn't attempt it any more for my own health. Of course, life can come at you fast, unless you're George Zimmerman, because we're still waiting. But if survival has become like drinking water, only two things are fundamentally important to your existence: staying Black and dying (lit).

Rapper, Actor, Athlete – Other
Black male identity and the colonial imaginary
JJ Bola

'I know what you're going to be when you're older, if you don't make it pro, that is. You'll become a PE teacher.' That's what one of my secondary-school teachers said when I was thirteen years old. I cringed at this thought, not because I saw anything wrong with becoming a PE Teacher – I enjoyed the subject, as most secondary-school children do – it was more because of his tone of voice; the certainty and absoluteness. As if subtly insinuating that there was nothing else I could be. As if I was predestined to play sports, or somehow work in sports, and could not be suited to or interested in any other domain – such as astrophysics; fulfilling the boyish curiosity about space that had kept me watching shows such as *Star Wars*, *Star Trek*, *Stargate SG1* and *Quantum Leap*, and always asking questions about the universe. Or perhaps a sociologist, considering how interested I was in society and the world from a young age. Or, arguably the most absurd of all, a writer of books, given how much I loved reading and writing stories as a child – which became the path that I eventually stumbled upon.

No. The path that had been laid out for me, according to my teacher at least, was sports. This conversation struck me even then, decades ago. I still remember, quite vividly, the visceral reaction that I had inside; although I held my tongue, I strongly rejected any suggestion that I could not be more than an athlete. It made me acutely aware of the gaping contrast between how I saw myself and how I was perceived, particularly in regard to being a young Black boy. How often, as a young Black boy, you were pigeonholed in the category of rapper, actor, athlete or other. Admittedly, I did love sports. Or rather, basketball. Sports were never really a thing that entirely interested me. I loved basketball growing up, particularly the NBA. It was one of the rare spaces where I saw Black men have such positive engagement with each other, while also making up the majority (the National Basketball Association is 80% Black – players, not ownership, which is another conversation). I watched Michael Jordan turn up to games in suits, a shirt and tie. I watched Kobe Bryant hold interviews in English, and then Italian, then Spanish. I watched the countless other basketball professionals, who had graduated from college, played professional sports, then gone on to pursue careers in other fields – all the while balancing education and sport, contrary to the clichéd supposition that they are mutually exclusive. I quickly learned that, for basketball in particular, doing well in school was linked to a potential career in the pros. This duality, or even multiplicity, allowed me to break out of and look beyond the stereotyping and pigeonholing, and take steps to construct an identity that was fitting for me.

There are certain rites of passage that are associated with being a young Black man, some that are imposed on you, as if from nowhere; some that bring you closer to being seen as a true representative of that identity; and others that leave you wondering if you fit into that identity at all, particularly if you are from an inner-city area. Some of these associations are, of course: being good at sport/naturally athletic (just think how the African/Black players are described in any sporting event, the World Cup for instance, compared to other players; 'pace' and 'power', on repeat). Having natural dancing ability and rhythm. 'Hood' or 'road(man)', or any other colloquialism that signifies inner-city, working class and poor, and has connotations of gangs, drugs, crime or violence. And, last but not least, to be quite blunt, having a large penis or insatiable sexual appetite. I've been confronted with each of these at certain points in my life — and I know most Black men will relate. At the work Christmas party, a simple two-step elicits the reaction, 'wow, JJ can really dance' (plot twist: I can't – I fake-dance a lot). While on a night out, someone will ask if I sell drugs. And perhaps, the most cringeworthy of all: being asked, 'Is it true what they say about Black men?' while pointing to (sometimes even grabbing) my phallic region.

There is an obsession in non-Black communities, for instance white or Asian, about the Black male penis. Often, the question that the women of those communities get asked is 'Do you like Black guys? or 'Have you been with a Black guy?', which is also a projection of the ongoing colonial mentality. These are the subtle acts of dehumanisation that reduce your body, your being, as a Black man, to an object; less than an object, to a thing void of soul. I often wondered what the origins of these stereotypical projections of Black maleness were. How people have sat so comfortably with these assumptions, to the point where they hold them as true, particularly if they've had very little interaction with the Black male identity. I started to look at how history influences the way we see the world today; especially in relation to various nations, cultures and identities. And, more specifically, to the history of colonialism. The Berlin Conference happened in 1884–5, in Germany. It was where powerful European nations such as Great Britain, France, Germany and Portugal met to decide which parts of the African continent would be prescribed as part of their colonies. Great Britain would gain control over

Nigeria, Ghana and Kenya – to name but a few; France over the Ivory Coast, Burkina Faso, Mali – to name but a few; Germany over Namibia, Tanzania – to name but a few.

The land of my ancestors, Congo, was given to the Belgian state, under the rule of Leopold II. Colonialism across the board was a brutal, dehumanising, genocidal, capitalist, exploitative venture. In Congo specifically, over 15 million people were killed during Leopold's rule, many of whom died as a direct result of the suffering endured on the rubber plantations, where the hands of Congolese were cut off if they didn't produce enough rubber. Not to mention the erasure of languages, religions, spiritual beliefs and cultures with the imposition of French and Catholicism as the official language and religion of the state.

Beyond that, one of the most impactful and long-lasting legacies of colonialism was the propaganda and misinformation that was spread about the oppressed peoples who were being subjugated; this occurred across the board during both European and Arab conquests. Let's look at how this expressly relates to the Black male identity. During the British colonial conquest in Kenya, the Mau Mau – resistance fighters who opposed colonial domination – were castrated and sexually abused under torture, as they were perceived to be lustful, lascivious and insatiable – because of their supposed large penises, an idea originating in the colonial imagination. Many Black and African men – that is to say Black men on the continent and Black men in the diaspora – were castrated, or even killed, as a result of this propaganda.

During the Belgian colonial era in the Congo, the comic series *Tintin in the Congo (Tintin au Congo*; 1931–46), featuring Tintin, an explorer, and his dog, Snowy, was very popular, particularly throughout the Francophone world. The series featured some of the most racist, xenophobic portrayals of people from all over the world, but particularly of the Congolese. In one of the earlier sketches, Tintin arrives in the Congo and is preparing for an expedition with Snowy. The scene goes as follows: 'We must make our preparations. We need a "boy" and a car.' 'And above all else, don't forget my mosquito net!' replies Snowy. 'So that's agreed, Coco. You'll accompany me throughout my journey in the Congo.' 'Yes, Master,' replies Coco. 'He doesn't look very bright!' says Snowy.

This is just one example of the very racist, western imperialist, superior attitude that came along with, or, rather, was at the root of, colonialism and the profiling of the Black male identity (which, of course, also included profiling Black women with an equal number of damaging stereotypes). It propagates the idea that there is a supposed natural hierarchy of the Belgian/European as the master (superior), and the Congolese or African as the slave (inferior). The Belgians even went so far as to all the Congolese who were educated, and could speak, read and write in French, *'les evolués'* – i.e. the evolved. Furthermore, that the Black or African person is of a lower class of intelligence even than dog – it is Snowy who makes the comment about not looking very bright. Throughout the comic series, Black/African people are depicted – not just in regards to stereotypical tropes, but also physically, using the 'golliwog' look, i.e. exaggeratedly large lips and tar-like black skin – in ways that dehumanise and reduce Black existence to the lowest colonial denominator. These ways were instituted across the education system and the media during European control. Furthermore, during slavery and the colonial era in Africa, in plantations and across the diaspora, Black people were forced to entertain, dance and perform for their slave masters, which had a twofold intention: to monitor the health of an enslaved African, and to maintain domination and control.

I often consider the extent to which these racist attitudes are reproduced in modern society, within institutions, schools and colleges, for example, and how they inform our everyday thinking and interactions. Did the teacher who was certain that I would have a career in sports make this assumption based on my ability or the reproduction of remnants of colonial ideas? That Black people are more suited to the physical than the intellectual, that a young Black male is better suited to playing sports than he is to writing. Now, of course – this goes without saying – I am not pitting one against the other, or saying one is more valuable than the other: athlete or writer, physical or intellectual. I do not see them as mutually exclusive. I'm merely asking why one is normalised over the other, in particular when it comes to the Black male identity.

One interesting aspect, which is often overlooked, is the subtle and nuanced differences in colonial propaganda and misinformation, depending on who the oppressor was, and how this influenced the identity of the colonised. Generally, each conquering nation perpetuated very similar methods of other-ness and oppression. Three international footballers of different Europeans nations, who come from immigrant backgrounds – Romelu Lukaku, Belgian player of Congolese descent; Karim Benzema, French player of Algerian descent; and Mesut Özil, German player of Turkish descent – have recently all concluded the same sentiment: that when they are successful, they are claimed by that European nation, but when they lose, they are linked to their country of origin. It's as if to subtly reinforce the idea that success, when in servitude of the state, can help you bypass the burden of your colonial or ethnic identity, and become part of the hegemony.

Being of Congolese descent but growing up in the United Kingdom allowed me to be aware of the subtle nuances of how Black identity was perceived across different colonial regions. Particularly interesting was how an aspect of my identity gave me privilege in the other place; that is to say, if I was in the UK and mentioned my francophone background, my treatment would be slightly elevated, and if I was in France and mentioned my anglophone background, I'd have a similar experience. However, this did not occur for those who remained within those same colonised territories – nor did it occur when and where my Black or African identity was the one that dominated. This exemplifies how much colonial attitudes are a projection of whatever people understand to be true, and not what necessarily *is* true.

You will find as a young Black male that there is very little room to navigate around these identities. Young Black men are socialised (sometimes pressured) into performing these roles, often not because of their own will, but because of what is expected of them. However, there is a large group, a whole subculture of young Black males, who grew up involved in cultures that wouldn't ordinarily be associated with Black men, such as anime, rock and alternative music, poetry, astrophysics, chess and so forth, much of which is becoming more widely visible because of social and independent media. Nonetheless, the change in representation and the impact on the Black male identity in society is slow to manifest.

There are two main things to consider. The first is the issue of double consciousness, a termed coined by African American sociologist and activist W. E. B. Du Bois which describes the internal conflict experienced by oppressed groups, a 'two-ness', a sense of always looking at oneself through the eyes of others. Secondly, there is the issue of the self-fulfilling prophecy, which is defined as a false definition of the situation, evoking new behaviour which makes the originally false conception come true. If we relate this to the colonial projections and impositions on the Black male identity – sexual insatiability and aggressiveness, athleticicism and violence – we can see how these stereotypes are perpetuated and exacerbated in the media's representation of Black males and how, in turn, these conceptions can become internalised by other people, and by young Black males themselves – who then experience an internal conflict, particularly if they do not have alternative depictions of their own identity which are closer to who they are.

Black male identity includes such a wide, diverse, nuanced existence that does not get represented in the media or seep into people's consciousness when they think of Black males – in many cultures around the world, from Africa to the Americas, across Europe and Asia, the West and the Global South: none are singular, but many are connected. When I think of my own experience navigating my Black male identity – particularly transitioning from boyhood to manhood – from my francophone Congolese origins, to my anglophone London upbringing, I can recall the many moments when I was pressured to perform or live up to an expected inner-city Black-maleness (just think of how many 'roadman' caricatures, which are essentially caricatures of Black men, have reached social-media popularity). Where this expectation was not met, there was often ridicule.

I can recall being called 'freshie', if my identity ventured too far in my Africanness – for instance, when I wore my dashiki tops – or being called 'posh', if my identity ventured too far with things that were associated with being white – such as reading. The irony was that it was my Blackness that informed both. In my culture, as I often explain to surprised friends, Congolese men are always expected to be well dressed; the culture of sapology and fashion is not gender-specific. So often, the way we dressed as teenagers, influenced by our Congolese heritage – traditional wear and bright colours – was not understood by peers. Nor was the way we danced. In Congolese culture, the men dance by engaging their hips and shaking their bums, which, to the outside eye, can appear 'effeminate' (for those who are curious, I will neither confirm nor deny whether I can dance like this). Just look at the older videos of Koffi Olomide and JB Mpiana dancing Ndombolo, or more recently, the likes of Fally

Ipupa or Fabregas (if these names and dances are unfamiliar to you – where have you been? – do check out a video, and entertain yourself for the day). However, these styles of dance are often misunderstood in the West, where there is a rigid view of the Black male identity. And across the world, there are other examples that differ from the widespread perception of the Black male identity. For instance, Black men in Nigeria and Uganda hold hands as a sign of brotherhood or deep friendship. Or the Wodaabe men of Niger participate in traditional beauty pageants (known as Gerewol), where they wear make-up, flashy outfits and dance to impress the women who are the judges.

Now more than ever, we need to challenge what is represented as the de facto Black male identity, particularly as there are so many examples that disprove the ridiculous categorisations: rappers such as Akala, who recently received an honorary doctorate from Oxford Brookes University; or Hardy Caprio, the twenty-two-year-old rapper, who graduated with a first-class degree in Finance from Brunel University. We need to vehemently reject the associations of aggressiveness and lasciviousness. We desperately need to construct a Black male identity that is free of the remnants of colonial impositions, and that does not reproduce the oppressive, hierarchical structures that come with them, such as homophobia and patriarchy. An identity that merges the pre-colonial Black male identity with the beautiful, yet too rarely discussed, cultures and positive representations of Black maleness that exist around the world, particularly in Africa and the Global South.

Now, I am not saying that these regions are completely free of the impositions of the colonial imagination; rather, I am saying that in many of these cultures, they are more closely connected to an authentic pre-colonial source. Liberation, freedom – true freedom – comes from self-determination, self-actualisation and agency; that is to say, the will and ability to choose for ourselves who we are, from our own imaginings, and bring that into being, while also having control over how we are seen by others. Until then, we may find ourselves continuously torn between the compound effect and internal conflict of battling who we are and who we are seen to be; navigating between both, in an attempt to survive in a world that poorly understands us.

We cannot afford to sit and wait. Things must change, and with urgency, lest we live in the shadows of colonialism for ever. It is our duty to provide a future for the generations to come, for as anti-apartheid activist Steve Biko said, 'Black man, you are on your own.'

I Have Two Fathers

Joseph Harker

I have two fathers.

The first was Nigerian, who came to Britain to study as an overseas student. He was in a relationship with my mum but disappeared as soon as he found out she was pregnant with me. The last time she saw him was the day she told him she was expecting his child.

My second father, who I call 'Dad', was a white dockworker who met my mum in Hull, East Yorkshire, when I was a toddler. She was Irish, a single parent and had a brown baby – three social stigmas back in the 1960s. Dad was regularly reminded of this, in the crudest of ways, by his work colleagues: Hull was a city in which, at that time, outsiders of any kind were rare. Yet despite the negative perceptions over their relationship, my Mum and Dad got married and, when I was six, he legally adopted me. He became my dad, not my stepdad, and I still carry his surname.

As a role model, you could say he wasn't the best: his job was fairly dead end, and he had no great desire for me to continue at school beyond sixteen, saying regularly that I should simply find 'manual work', in the way he and his father had done (and, no doubt, generations of his family before that, too). It was my mother who was always pushing for me to get a strong education, go to a good school and, after that, to university. Yet his wages put a roof over our heads, he took me to swimming lessons, to my first football matches, and drove us on family holidays. Right until my parents separated, in my late teens, he was there as a part of my life. He, not my birth father, was the one who taught me what being a dad really means.

Despite all Dad's love and care – which, being a child, I never fully appreciated at the time – I grew up with a deep sense of shame about being born 'out of wedlock' and of not knowing my 'real' father. In that era, there were so many negative perceptions of single motherhood and illegitimacy. In fact, it was not till after graduating, moving to London, and gaining my first job – at Black newspaper *The Voice* – that I realised my story was more common than I'd imagined. Many colleagues had been raised alone by their mothers; for some, of mixed-parentage like me, this meant by their white parent.

I was happy to know I wasn't alone, and to be able to talk to others in similar situations. And it certainly helped me accept there was no reason to feel shame. But at the same time, I wondered at the potential damage caused by the lack of fathers in so many lives.

This was the 1980s, when UK Black culture was dominated by the Caribbean and, in particular, Jamaican identity. It concerned me that there was such an acceptance of this model of parenting; that somehow the menfolk could impregnate women and then disappear, or at best play a minor, semi-detached role in their child's upbringing.

My own childhood had given me two models of fatherhood and it was clear to me which one was preferable. The security of having two parents in a committed relationship, all of us living under one roof, provided a solid building block for everything I did: be it schoolwork, friendships or any outside activities.

I'm not some puritanical tyrant who believes that all parents must be married, or that loveless or, worse, abusive relationships must be tolerated for the sake of the children. But I do feel fathers, especially Black fathers, should be encouraged to play a full role in the lives of their children. And I'm not sure that's happening.

Look at the figures: according to the Office for National Statistics (based on the 2011 Census), Black parents with dependent children are more likely than any other ethnic group to be single. In fact, there are as many lone-parent Black homes as there are married and cohabiting-couple households combined.[1] By comparison, five times more Asian households with dependent children are headed by a married couple than by a lone parent. And for white people it's two-and-a-half times that.

There's a history to this, of course. There's the famous phrase 'It takes a village to raise a child', popularised by Hillary Clinton in the 1990s, but thought to originate in Africa. Its usage is clearly well-meaning: for successful development, the child needs help not only from the immediate family but from the extended family and the local community. Yet somehow the message is often distorted: as if the immediate family doesn't matter that much. That there's a benign, willing group out there who can and will do just as much for the child as its parents. Given the mother is traditionally the child's primary carer, this makes the role that fathers play, and especially Black fathers, less crucial. Where is the father in this idealist 'village'? Is his role optional?

Added to this, centuries of brutality – first through slavery, then through colonialism and most recently via the racism of the state and its enforcers – have targeted Black men, above all. At worst leaving them dead or incarcerated; yet far more likely, leaving them unable to provide for their families due to low wages or high unemployment. While the Black man has been brutalised, subjugated or humiliated (a common story from

Africa to the Americas to Europe), the Black mother has been left to take care of the home, to be responsible for the children and, in many cases, for the household income, too.

The tale of the 'strong Black woman' has been told for generations. The superwoman who can do it all. Again, this is a positive story: in times of hardship and often, over the years, destitution, we need to cling to the idea that we have the innate power and energy to overcome all obstacles and win through. Yet once more it leaves little place for the role of Black men in the home. Is the Black mother so strong she needs no help? Is the Black father to be a peripheral figure?

And of course this is one stereotype that some men are only too keen to play along with. If they have no role in raising their child, they can do what they like: carry on enjoying life in their own carefree way, the perpetual free spirit, with none of the responsibilities that come with parenthood. No need to waste time taking your child to school, helping with the homework, the cooking, if the strong woman can do everything. Instead, just spend more time having fun with your mates.

For some Black men it's been a win–win. You can call yourself a 'baby father', which implies you have some role in your child's life, yet this can be as little as you like: from the minimum of sending birthday and Christmas presents, to doing the odd spot of childcare. All of which leave the child feeling disconnected from this key figure in its life. Recent history has taught us that, in this vacuum, children can often be attracted to gangs as their proxy father-figure – learning all the wrong lessons about being a man.

In the past few years there's been heated discussion about this issue: whether Black fathers really are absent from families; and if so, whether it's really a problem. Barack Obama himself, when a presidential candidate in 2008, weighed in with his own thoughts: 'Too many fathers [are] missing from too many lives and too many homes.' He was attacked for this by, among others, the Black US writer Ta-Nehisi Coates, who countered: 'From the White House on down, the myth holds that fatherhood is the great antidote to all that ails Black people.'[2]

Coates, though, is using a straw-man argument: no one claims better fatherhood would eradicate racism. The argument is simply that in dealing with systemic discrimination, stronger Black families would have greater resilience.

Having said that, it probably didn't help that the then Conservative party leader David Cameron leaped on to Obama's words to criticise Black fathers: 'We will never solve the long-term problems unless people also take responsibility for their own lives.'[3] For those of us wanting more Black fathers to recon-nect with their children, the last thing we need is for them to feel lectured by a right-wing white politician whose party has shown little interest in ending racial inequality.

But white liberals too have, in my view, been part of the problem. They like the idea of the strong single mother: the woman who's ditched her no-good man and now does things on her own, free from the overbearing and ungrateful patriarch. Yet many of the women they envision, from their middle-class perspective, are financially independent, highly educated and have the resources to compensate for the lack of a second parent: the childcare, the nanny, the school tutors, their own wealthy parents. They ignore the fact that, across Britain, almost half of children in single-parent families live in relative poverty, and face twice the risk of relative poverty compared to children in couple families.[4]

It's this combination of single parenthood and poverty that can have such a damaging impact on life chances. Feminists have done well to end the stigma of single motherhood – clearly, if one compares a mother raising a child alone with the absent father then there can only be one hero and one villain. Yet there's a danger in overcompensating, in which case the single parent becomes almost the ideal.

For all the talk about strong mothers, in the modern world – especially in the West – parenting is a crucial job and one person, however gifted, will struggle to do it by themselves. With stressful jobs, time and money pressures and a multitude of commitments, even for two parents it's often a stretch to give children all the attention they need. Homework alone needs constant monitoring, as does ensuring teachers are doing the best for your child, simply getting your child to school is never enough. And then, to give your child the best start in life, there's the after-school activities: be it sport, music or other cultural interests. They all take a lot of time to organise each week. And whether the second parent simply provides the money for this, or ideally the hands-on help too, their role is significant.

Yes, it's possible that one super-strong, wealthy and well-connected woman can do all this. But what about the average woman, for whom the ability to hold down a half-decent job and provide the most basic needs for her family is itself a struggle? This is why the role of the Black father, the second parent, is so important – in bringing on the next generation and giving them the best chance to build on the achievements of their parents.

Then there's the quality time with your child: in the park, at the movies, meeting friends and family. All the things that give a youngster that sense of being cared for, and part of a strong unit in which they can feel secure. And in which the parents' values can be passed on.

Which brings us to that crucial element of any child's upbringing: love. It's clear that being loved is a hugely influential element of how a child forms its identity – its sense of value and self-worth. Yet many Black children are raised to be 'tough' rather than loved; the Caribbean or African father who uses a belt to beat his errant child is legendary. Sometimes it feels as if this has become a model all Black fathers should aspire to. Given the past, it's not surprising how this brutal figure has emerged – 'it's a harsh world out there and you need to learn to cope with it' – and let's not forget, it's been part of Western fatherhood too. But in today's village-less world, resilience should instead be built up from strong, tender relationship bonds.

It still grieves me every time I see a young Black child on the train or bus, its face beaming with excitement at the world around it, yet with a parent totally disengaged – on the phone, or just disinterested. 'For God's sake, talk to your child,' I mutter under my breath. These are important moments for the infant to learn about humanity and relationships, yet the lessons it is receiving are purely negative. Is this the kind of parent, I ask, who will read the child a bedroom story each night, or give it a sense of wonder? There's already plenty of evidence of how reading has an influence on children's future life outcomes, and research in April 2018 showed that half of Britain's five-year-olds have such a limited vocabulary it harms their learning.[5]

Fatherhood, indeed parenthood, cannot be based on brutality and discipline: warmth and caring are what we should all aspire to. Thankfully, though, it seems the message is getting through that men should be bearing more responsibility. Recently we've seen more and more media stories giving a positive message about Black fatherhood. In one, twenty-three-year-old Cameron Scott-Marchant, told the *Guardian*: 'I know what it's like to grow up without a dad. It's not easy and it's not easy for the mum either. How could I walk away? . . . I don't want that for my girlfriend.' Scott-Marchant is one of the many young men taking advantage of a project for fathers and fathers-to-be, aged between fourteen and twenty-five, run by the St Michael's Fellowship in south London.[6]

Similarly, Sylvester Alebioshu, the father of an adult son, Samuel, told Buzzfeed: 'I feel responsible for how [my son] turns out as a man. . . . To be a good father, you need to be understanding, you need to have integrity, and you need to be honest. It's important that your child knows you, and you know your child. This is why I spend so much time with him.'[7] Stories such as these give me hope for the future.

I grew up with two fatherly role models: one showed me what a father can do if positively engaged in his child's life. The other became more of a cautionary tale: of what goes wrong when the father is absent; what kind of pressures it places on a mother; and all the things a child can miss out on.

For years, the conventional wisdom was that the mistakes of one generation are passed down to the next: that the children of a 'broken home' are destined to carry on the cycle of pain and hurt. And yet, as I'm starting to see with some younger Black men today, the absence of a father can create in them a will to correct the injustice; to ensure the same mistakes are not repeated; and to ensure their own children do not miss out on what they themselves did.

For the sake of our future generations, we need this new father figure to replace the old one.

_____

1 https://www.ethnicity-facts-figures.service.gov.uk/ethnicity-in-the-uk/ethnicity-and-type-of-family-or-household

2 https://www.theatlantic.com/magazine/archive/2014/06/the-case-for-reparations/361631/

3 https://www.theguardian.com/politics/2008/jul/16/davidcameron.conservatives1

4 https://www.gingerbread.org.uk/policy-campaigns/publications-index/statistics/

5 https://www.independent.co.uk/news/education/education-news/child-vocabulary-literacy-reading-word-primary-schools-a8311676.html; https://www.theguardian.com/books/2014/mar/11/survey-class-divide-reading-habits

6 https://www.theguardian.com/lifeandstyle/2013/mar/23/proud-young-black-fathers

7 https://www.buzzfeed.com/tolanishoneye/daddycool?utm_term=.gn41MAbmv#.sj9qLDmVx

The Good Bisexual

Musa Okwonga

I must admit that it feels as if there is a danger to writing this essay. Since the suffering which it describes came so long ago, has subsided so much, I am worried that I will not do it justice – that the reader may think that coming out as a bisexual Black man is not all that traumatic, that it is only in the head, that things are so easy these days. But then I remind myself that it is not my fault if I do not convey that pain so well; because, as many queer people know, the trauma of coming out can be so extreme that your body often defends you from all memory of it, making you blank out whole weeks and even years of that period when you thought the world was ending. If I don't capture accurately just how hard this road has been, then that is only partly due to my lack of ability as a writer, and mostly due to the fact that my own soul does not trust me to remember.

The realisation that I was bisexual came like a gradual change in the daylight; so gently that the first few times I looked, I could have sworn it was still mid-afternoon, but some time later I was in the middle of the plunging dusk. Aged twenty-one, I was walking down the street at university with my then girlfriend of eighteen months, when we caught sight of a boy and a girl approaching us. The couple were students like us, of British Asian heritage, confident and strikingly attired. The girl was beautiful, but the man – the man – he was —

'Cool', my mind reassured me. 'Cool'.

And I thought no more of it for two months; until I went home that summer, and one afternoon found myself idly watching daytime television with my twelve-year-old sister. A series of adverts cantered across the screen, and my sister voiced her thoughts on the attractiveness of the different men diligently plugging their products before her. 'He's fit,' she declared; then, moments later, 'He's fit, he's fit'. There was nothing remarkable about this – only that, to my horror, I agreed with my sister's assessment. Unknown to her, we were both going through a form of puberty at the same time.

Queer puberty can seem so humiliating: so many of us are late starters that we feel hapless, hopelessly exposed. Because the world still works to make us overwhelmingly ashamed of same-sex attraction, it often takes LGBTI people far longer than heterosexual people to acknowledge our sexuality: and so we find ourselves in nightclubs, in our mid- to late- twenties, as bumbling and awkward as teenagers who've not yet had their first kiss. And that's before the issue of race came into it, which – in my case at least – multiplied the discomfort in ruthless fashion.

I can't speak for all bisexual Black men; I can only say my path to self-acceptance has frequently been a brutal one, and that my skin colour has been a huge factor in that. In popular culture, Black men are continually depicted as vast, unthinking thugs. We are widely seen as being inherently criminal, an entire class of wasters. Stigmatised as such, we can find ourselves taking refuge in another unfortunate stereotype – that we represent true masculinity in all its potency and swagger, the outlaws who still emerge on top. As ridiculous as that sounds, it makes every kind of sense. It's a defence mechanism against all those times, from the age of twelve or younger, you start getting picked out of crowds by police, or targeted for confrontation by older, taller white men. Black hypermasculinity was the reward, the payback, for all the racism that had come my way and that was to come: the knowledge that I was a Black Man, and Black Man did not get fucked over – or fucked – by anyone.

Within all this, though, there was obviously a problem. The damaging effects of racism and homophobia are often compared – mainly by people who have experienced only one or neither of those torments. Having endured both, I can say that homophobia felt different to me in one respect: the day I finally accepted I was attracted to men, it was if a landmine had gone off in my soul. A landmine which I and countless others – the authors of the Bible, my classmates, my favourite rappers, the odd family member, chat-show host, newspaper headline writer and passer-by – had patiently assembled over the first two decades of my life – and so devastating was that explosion, fashioned by so many people and elements of culture that I loved, that I am astonished that I survived it.

I survived, but it seemed that everything I had going for me was dying. First went my relationship of two years, with a woman so kind and beautiful that I knew there had to be a catch from the moment I met her. There was no way a guy like me could have ended up with a girl like that. Then went my grades – before I sat my exams at law school, I had already secured a job offer from one of London's most prestigious law firms, but my results were so awful in that term's tests that I put my career in jeopardy. My future employers, looking on from London, must have been confused – how was someone who had routinely delivered excellent marks now struggling with the most basic of trials? Finally, I withdrew in shame from my family and friends. I was living alone at that time, and for the first few nights after I broke up with my girlfriend I would lie awake and hammer my head against the wooden headboard at the top of my bed, as if by doing so I could beat the gayness out. But the homosexuality was in every part of me, in every cell – it had only been a few months, but I could sense it. Bruised and exhausted, I would eventually pass out, only for the torment to begin again the next day. This state continued, with about the same level of intensity, for three whole years: an intensely private and violent shame, rumbling along behind every conversation.

And I knew that this was my punishment. For years I had feared that I was doomed to fall – that there had to be a price for my success. Who the hell did I think that I was? My mother, widowed after my father's death in a war far abroad, had raised five of us by herself in West Drayton, a small working-class suburb near Heathrow Airport. From there, I had won scholarships to prestigious private schools and then a place at one of the world's leading universities – something had to go wrong, I thought. And this was it. Being gay was my grand downfall.

Except it wasn't – not really. Not at all, in fact. Because acceptance from others came in surprising ways. When I told one friend, who had been raised in a similarly conservative home, he simply looked at me and replied: 'Ah, that explains it. I thought something was up. You do realise,' he continued – with startling wisdom – 'that now everyone needs to know.' His reasoning was that, knowing me, I would not cope very well with my sexuality being an open secret; that it was best to face the world, the relatively progressive setting of my university town, exactly as I was. And so, a few days later, I turned up at a meeting of Oxford's LGBT society, my first public outing – so to speak – as a Black gay man. I like to think that I appeared as nonchalant as can be, even though I was as nervous as I had ever been.

Slowly – painfully slowly – I found myself again. For the first eighteen months after I came out, I didn't sleep with a man. Instead, I spent that time mostly reading, researching, finding out as much as I could about the gay people who had come before me. I had been taught by society that to be gay was to be evil, a feeling so insistent that for the next few years I could barely listen to the lyrics of my favourite emcees, littered as they were with homophobic references. All of a sudden, they weren't talking about some abstract hate figures – when they talked about faggots, they were now talking directly about me. This is the key reason why I am now such a huge fan of several genres of music – because the horror of being taunted by my musical heroes was so great that I stopped listening to any music with lyrics, and sought solace in liquid drum and bass, dubstep, techno, trance and classical.

Meanwhile, I had to reprogramme myself, to remind myself that I was still human. And so I dived into the works of James Baldwin, Allan Gurganus and Audre Lorde, discovering the heritage of the bold, playful or just simply persistent queer people who had travelled this path before me and somehow made my path that little bit easier. I joined Stonewall FC, a team for gay and bisexual men in London, and the sense of fellowship I found there lasts to this day.

In particular, among the club's hundred or so members, I met Aislie, Peter, Tony and Jules, four Black men living their lives with pretty much the same ups and downs as any heterosexual people. In short, for the inspiring and matter-of-fact manner in which they approached each day, they immediately became my role models. (They still are.) It took me a further year-and-a-half to summon the courage even to kiss a man – before then, I feared that I would come away from the experience hating myself – and when I finally did so, in that famous old pub called The Swan, down in Limehouse, my housemate Peter hugged me.

'Congratulations', he said, 'I'm so happy for you'.

I was so happy and proud at how far I had come, so overwhelmed by the length of the journey, that I could have burst into tears.

During the next few years, I had my fair share of flings – in short, how many people, gay, bi or straight, spend their mid-twenties with love proving elusive? Somewhere along the way, at the age of around twenty-eight, I attended a house party and ended up kissing a woman, and we saw each other for a month; after which, to my friends' amusement, I bashfully announced that I thought I might in fact be bisexual.

'Of course you are,' one of them said. 'We were waiting for you to work that out.'

That's not to say that there weren't drawbacks along the way. Some of my close relatives were less than keen on my revelation, meaning that I barely attended family gatherings for several years. There was the time one of my work colleagues, aware of my discomfort at my sexuality, taunted me about being gay during a seminar; and the time one of our firm's biggest clients went on a prolonged homophobic rant, just after he had signed a major contract with us. There were times where heterosexual housemates, if everyday situations became tense, lashed out at my sexuality with barely hidden contempt. There was also the immediate fear of what would happen if I was identified as gay in a hostile environment – and the occasion when, on a bus back to Croydon, I was attacked by a group of young men after sticking up for another queer person on the bus.

It was rough; and it was made all the worse by the sense, that, even though I had come out, I still didn't feel as if my new identity fitted me. I don't mean in some macho sense – I was thankfully past that stage. It was more that I privately suspected that I still liked women, but I didn't know if that was just an advanced state of denial. And so it was that, between the ages of twenty-two and twenty-eight, I was pretty much convinced that I didn't exist. Bisexual Black men, so far as I knew, were a thing of myth, and so any thought that I might be one of them was ridiculous. Bisexuality wasn't real, in my view. From what I had read, from what I had been continually taught, it was merely a stepping stone from straight to gay, a label men and women used while growing more comfortable with their attraction to the same sex. An L-plate for gays, if you will. How, I wondered, could sexuality be on a spectrum? How, when the sensation of sleeping with men and with women was so different?

Friends told me I was bisexual long before I saw it myself. Maybe, looking back, it was the identity that I was most afraid to accept. Because a lot of people don't seem to have a lot of use for bisexual men. We are frequently seen as untrustworthy, as men who will blend into the heterosexual background as soon as the stigma of homosexuality gets too great. As a result of these perceptions, I have been open about my sexual orientation in my work, but I fully understand those who are not. Years ago, I was offered work experience at a local council in London, but when a close relative discovered that one of the employees was queer – a Black man who, by all accounts, was one of the most popular and accomplished members of staff – I was barred from attending. When I came out of the closet, I knew that I was now that person, that kind queer man who some young Black boy would never meet. That realisation was devastating.

I also understand that coming out represents a gamble, one whose odds are often too great to bear. You are essentially saying that, in telling the world who you truly are, you will still have what it takes to thrive both personally and professionally. Looking around me even a few years ago, I saw very few openly gay or bisexual Black men in the fields where I worked. That remains the case now, in the worlds of music, poetry, political journalism and football writing. I will never know what opportunities I may have lost – and, more positively, may have gained – through being frank about who I am.

I don't mind that so much, because I look at being a bisexual Black man a little like a father or mother might look at their children – you endure all the suffering that you can in order to make it easier for the next generation. The greatest initial fear of mine, and an occasionally recurring one, was that I had disappointed and embarrassed my family – that my sexuality would negate all of my other achievements. After all, I come from an ethnic group – the Acholi, from northern Uganda – which has endured two genocides under successive dictators (Idi Amin in the 1970s, and Yoweri Museveni, the country's current president, in the 1980s). The cultural expectation was that I would go into a well-paid job, have a family and thereby become a respected member of the community – and my choice of career and my choice to live my life honestly have threatened to negate both of those.

I know that my writing is respected by many from my community, yet I maintain a certain distance in everyday life. I think that this is sensible, given the hostility orchestrated by the Ugandan government against queer people: you just never know how much of that hostility is shared by millions of others of Ugandan heritage, and so I keep myself scarce in those spaces, just in case. Viewing matters now, I can say that I have made a good life for myself; but I can't forget those who haven't, who still struggle with significant and silent torment. I know they are out there, because of the confessions of same-sex experiences my friends make to me after a few drinks; because of the lack of openly bisexual people in my family and in the wider Black community, in the worlds of politics, entertainment and sport. I know that the barriers to coming out are still very much there, because of the way in which I have taken a step back from the public sphere in order to find my happiness.

There remains a sense in which this is a subject that goes largely undiscussed; that my sexual orientation is on the whole to be tolerated, rather than celebrated. Much as there are newcomers to a country who feel they must prove themselves to the host population through acts of skill, intellect or bravery – marking them out as 'the good immigrants' – I am probably, in many eyes, 'the good bisexual'. I am friendly and hardworking and outgoing: for many who still have prejudice against bisexual people, I am easy to like, despite who I might date, sleep with or even love. Fortunately, though, I have now found my own island of happiness, as have so many queer people before me, populated only by those who care about me deeply. And from here, with care and determination, I will try to help to nudge the world forward.

The Sticks

Aniefiok 'Neef' Ekpoudom

A boy lived on the outer edges of south London, on the rim of a wide, steep valley about fifteen miles from Big Ben. The skyscrapers that loomed over central London's city streets had long faded to green farmland and, looking from his bedroom window, he could see kettled suburban housing smoothed over low-lying flatlands, like butter over bread rolls. Orpington was officially Kent in 1965. Then vague laws were rafted through parliament, the home counties conceded to the capital, and a stale commuter town, with bleak horizons and no tube station, was swallowed whole by Greater London. And so now, in 2018, red buses skim the slow-moving avenues and coast along residential backstreets. They skate past Morley's, on the high-street corner, and then gently rumble down the rest of the narrow road which is lined with charity shops and white boys peddling battered BMXs.

He lived at the top of a hill, with his parents and twin brother. They were a West African family, skin dark, noses wide, lips full, the first on the street when the moving truck offloaded their possessions in 2001. It was the great Black migration south: Lewisham to Bromley, city to suburb, council estate to his own room and a green garden with a patio and a shed; the immigrants' dream, reality reimagined, family and financial stability from cleaning jobs and waiting tables.

During that same year, he began at his new primary school. In the early autumn, on the first day of term, he stood nervously at the front of the class, fidgeting with his fingers, staring out into the sea of puzzled white faces. Until that moment, he had never known to register race. But he saw no resemblance of himself in the eyes that stared back at him, could hear the teacher struggling to curl her lips around his Nigerian name, and he somehow felt that his early years of no creed, no colour had been a blissful lie. Later that morning, in a case of mistaken identity, after a student had scribbled on the blackboard, the teacher grabbed the boy's wrist, her face scarlet, her voice serious, and screamed at him, 'Don't bring any of your Lewisham rubbish into our school!'

It was a splintering of innocence, a nine-year old's discovery that utopia was reserved for the scriptures, that Santa was only fiction, the tooth fairy a fabrication, the Easter bunny make-believe. In that moment – when his naïvety shattered like glass and crumbled to the classroom floor – the veil had briefly been lifted and he had snatched a glimpse of the Western world as it had always seen him – the other, the undesirable.

Surprisingly, after this incident with the teacher, race did not come to dominate those early years, but more ambled on in the background, and he soon settled into suburban south London, making friends, visiting their homes and welcoming them into his. During the weekends and the long summer holidays, when the gardens were green, the lawns were manicured and the sun burned brightly on the horizon, they chased footballs and Frisbees, and cooled off with water guns and the cold spray from yellow garden hoses. It marked what was altogether an enjoyable period, during which it became apparent that despite the teacher, he and the other children had not yet learned to hate or to separate one another along the lines of race or class or religion. So, much of his childhood in the suburban no man's land, the anonymous halfway house mired amid London and Kent, continued in this fashion. Confined to the four walls of home, in his own private kingdom of gardens and playgrounds, the two years that preceded secondary school were chapters of prolonged shelter, and his innocence, though irretrievably spoiled, did not suffer any further damaging blows. But true freedom lives outside, and the world he had first glimpsed that one morning in Year 5 still lay in wait on his doorstep.

I struggle to pinpoint the high-water mark regarding the painful departure from the ecstasy of infant bliss, and the incident that first reintroduced me to the scorn of being Black in London's home-county borders. Perhaps there were too many to recall. But I do remember that it started around 2004, in secondary school, with a cocktail of fear and isolation.

My first secondary school had been a multiracial, multicultural all-boys Comprehensive, just outside Orpington, where students came from Lewisham and Grove Park, Bexley and Bromley, all testosterone-fuelled, all dressed in black blazers and black shoes. Through rebellion, we felt out the world and our early places among it. Classes were sometimes as big as sixty, boundaries were leaned on, fighting was frequent, and so those first school terms, in the autumn of Year 7, seemed to endure with a prevailing sense of lawlessness.

We roamed the school fields, stalked the hallways, roved through the canteen like wild jackal. Bullying became regular, ignorant bundles and beatings for those who had dare drift from the norm, grungers and goths rushed in the hallways before music lessons, a penalty to pay for splintering from the mob, unkindly judged for their daring to be different, but never for their race. If the older kids foreshadowed our steps, then this no-race, no-religion pre-teen swarm could only be temporary. The Year 10s and Year 11s were fractured, separate, more measured: white boys rarely mixed with Black boys, Black boys rarely mixed with white boys. Turkish boys mixed with neither; distant realities that collided only briefly during shoving matches by the lockers, a seemingly inevitable conclusion for my immediate future.

But I was pulled from the school early in Year 8, parent orders, a third fresh start in as many years, a brave bid to find the straight road in a fourth school. The grounds at this new place were larger and the uniform was blue rather than black. The student size remained the same, but now half were girls, and nearly all were white. Then one afternoon about a year in, while riding the red bus home, an older kid barrelled down the stairs with his friend, looked around the packed lower deck, and then into my eyes, and said, 'Oh my God, I see a Black boy! . . . Coon . . . Coon . . . you Black bastard.' They both left, laughing as the back doors opened, then closed, and I remember suddenly feeling alone, feeling the eyes from the blue-blazers settling on my face, wishing to be home, suffering in silence.

The tableside chats with my parents regarding racism had largely concerned institutional matters, obsessive reminders that both myself and my brother would have to outrun and outwork our white peers to see parity. The sentiment had filtered deep into my psyche. In school, I achieved well, studied hard; and when engaged, enjoyed good relationships with my teachers. But this vigorous preparation for life in the exam hall, and in the workplace – though valuable – had no bearing on, nor readied me in any way for, life on the street. A high-scoring English essay was no defence from a racial tirade, a successful Maths exam no barrier from being labelled a 'Black bastard' as I made my way home.

Racism became a stark reminder that I was somehow different, a relentless, isolating experience that separated a fourteen-year-old boy from the rest of his peers. At an age where the thirst for approval is bested in importance only by the need for water and shelter, the brutal cursing of my dark skin became a plague on the mind, eroded a fragile sense of self-worth, stripped me of morale, festered fear and anxiety. Deep-seated insecurities corrupted juvenile joy. I felt myself wander down an inevitable path, shunning blind trust and a belief in the goodness of people for suspicion and scepticism.

Our adolescent years are a gradual breakdown of these values. We fall from grace into adulthood, displace unconditional love of others and ourselves for a reality that is restricted, bargained for with fear. We learn to shutter from those who have hurt us and those who may do so in the future. Inadequacies gnaw at the skin. We hide like thieves in the night. I covered up, scrambled into my shell, never mentioned the questions around community and belonging that beleaguered my spirit, drove chasms between myself and my neighbours. It was a lonely existence. I remember wondering whether my home, anchored on the road to nowhere, on the edges of the garden county and the capital, somehow compromised my Blackness, and I also remember desperately wishing that I had been raised in a town with an SE postcode, so much so that I stuttered whenever a stranger enquired after my origins, always mumbling quietly, but never confidently, that 'I *live* in Orpington but I was *born* in Lewisham.'

How could home hate me? How could I be Blacker? How could I fade to the background in a town where I so distinctly stood out?

These are questions without answers when you are young and afraid. For the victim, there is no pattern to racism. Incidents sweep along by chance, at random, casually like the wind. Often, for myself at least, they occurred on the street, with the drivers of passing cars and vans spitting out slurs and waving fists and beating their horns. The vehicles would slow, the driver cutting his eyes, baring teeth, his face washed with embittered hatred for a soul he had never met but was certain that he loathed. The assaults came in a blitz of shouting and screaming, more personal than political, 'Niggers' and 'Monkeys', 'Coons' and 'Black Cunts', a mask for their own anxieties. Then they would screech off in a waft of smoke and my heartrate would slow, the jitters would remain, and I would continue with my journey.

There were also incidents that gave cause for more serious concern. One summer afternoon, while I climbed the hill to home, a man steering the wheel of a white van spotted me on the pavement. His face turned cherry. The van veered suddenly into my path. I went stiff. He kissed the curb, then straightened back into the road. Gone. On a separate evening, a band of boys cornered me at the exit of a kebab shop and spat 'Nigger!' as I searched for an escape. I was fourteen, the same year in which my computer was hacked at school, the work erased, swapped with a single document titled 'Go Back to Africa you dirty NIGGER!!' Not even the beautiful game was sacred. At the football matches during lunchtime, kids made monkey noises whenever the ball touched my feet.

Racism shadowed my steps. She subtly surfaced in the parks and in the schools, in the summer and in the spring. It was a reminder that regardless of how I dressed or spoke, the sports I played or the friends I kept, in this corner of the capital where horizons were sheltered and the valleys sharp, I would find no shelter, no place to call home.

Regrettably, there is little that can be done to shift the psyches of those who have been taught to hate from the womb, who shake their fists from vans, who corner small boys outside of kebab shops. Because racism is a learned trait, passed down from parent to child like a last name or a piece of gold. Those who taunted me during school have moved from blue blazers to labouring jobs and building sites, from the parks into the pubs.

So now, my heart sometimes still quickens slightly whenever a white van slowly cruises past on a quiet street. I find myself scowling when alone and I catch the eye of a bands of boys at the back of a bus or train – a masquerade, concealing the flutters in my stomach with a stone-face mask. It's as if I were still fourteen and afraid. Life has a wicked way of keeping the cruel experiences with you. A moment in the eyes can last a lifetime in the mind. Paranoia became my battle scar. Throughout my teens, I trod my path through Orpington carefully – sometimes still avoid notorious estates, hang my hood over my eyes when passing through certain neighbourhoods, always vigilant, scanning the streets, plotting my path home like a black cab driver picks his way through the West End.

But racists no longer roam the roads in Orpington, and Black boys and white boys float freely together across the town. The reports of racial strife and assault are now infrequent, and the great migration south continues. A Black community has emerged from the West African and West Indian families scattered across the valley. The Black barbershop – across the street from a pub – is filled from the early hours to the late evening. In the winter, we fetch Maggi and Milo from the 'African shop'. Summer barbeques smell of Puff-Puff and plantain. Orpington is now home, and my old wounds have healed.

But they had healed before the town staggered into twenty-first century London, before the barbershops and the barbeques. It happened sometime around twenty, a stumble from fear, a yield to innocence, a slow-burning revelation that a life imprisoned by the perception of others is no life at all. Perhaps I had become numb to it all. Whatever it was, I have now come to feel a strange, though fleeting, sense of sympathy for my aggressors. Because they too have fallen from grace into adulthood. But more deeply than most of us. They are prisoners to their own narrow perceptions, walled off from the wider world, caged by their own fear and suspicion; and in doing so, they have missed out on life, seen society through only one lens, watched the flowers bloom in only black and white. It is a starved existence, so much so that they can only gaze with contempt and wave their fists when they see skin that is dark and noses that are wide and lips that are full.

The last time I was stared at with such venom was earlier this week, not far from my home and where the white van had threatened to mow me down summers ago. But now it was a cold February in Orpington, and everything was bright and frosty. I had embarked on a brisk walk to the train station, striding over frozen cracked pavements and narrow roads skirted by maisonettes and terraced homes, and as the green valley dipped beneath a clear but cold sky, I could see a jeep climbing the hill.

The driver was a middle-aged man, white but with features I cannot recall. These encounters no longer seem to stick as they once had. For a few moments, we crossed paths, strangers on a lonely road, and as the jeep slowed, through the windshield I could see the toxic stare that had terrorised my childhood. But I felt no heart beating loudly in my chest, no sweat on my palm, no panic in my step. He passed by my side, tilting his head through the window, watching until our eyes met. I turned and caught his gaze. He glared, and I smiled.

Prisoner to the Streets: A Mentality

Robyn Travis

It's ironic that I'm an author now and spend my days writing. I wasn't academic growing up. Truth be told, I was the exact opposite and got expelled from multiple secondary schools. In class, I was either daydreaming, bussin' jokes or being sent out for being disruptive. The first time I read a book, I was eighteen and in prison in Jamaica. It was Malcolm X's autobiography and it moved me in a way I can't describe. Never in a million years did I think I would become an author myself. It wasn't even a consideration, especially coming from where I was coming from. But the pen chose me and I was compelled to write my memoir, *Prisoner to the Streets*. It wasn't easy, not just because I'm dyslexic and was homeless through a lot of the writing process, but because the title sums up a mentality which is literally killing our young people and, as much as I wanted to move away from my past, I also felt an unrelenting need to use my experiences to help our future generations save themselves.

So when I say a *Prisoner to the Streets*, what do I mean?

A Prisoner to the Streets (PTTS) is a person who is imprisoned in his or her own mind. This mindset results in a person displaying certain behavioural patterns which keep them trapped in a vicious cycle of violence and a self-destructive mindset of accepting road-life as a way of life. Accepting that this is the way life goes rather than this is the way we make it. Some people on the streets have been given or identify themselves as a 'roadman'. But as of recently, I have become uncomfortable with this term. I lived and was willing to die for this 'roadman mentality' myself. Until I discovered through harsh experiences that a roadman and a man of integrity are two different things. And after years of conflict with self, I now firmly believe that a 'roadman' can't teach a young boy much about being a 'stand-up man'.

Now the old me wouldn't like that statement at all, and he'd probably argue that the statement isn't true. The old me would most likely get defensive about his roadman values and belief and argue with the present me, saying something like: 'What are you on about, cuz? I know nuff man out here providing for their families . . . These same man work on the road daily. Forget a 9 to 5, they working from 9 to 9 just to feed their yutes [children]. These same men clothe them, pay bills, and they even put a little money in Mummy's purse here and there. So who are you to say that a roadman can't teach a boy to be a man?'

Now, the me of today smiles to myself at that argument, realising that the younger me makes some good points, and yet he fails to see the bigger picture. When I hear this kind of thing from young people, I try to respond in a way which isn't patronising, as I was once at that place in my journey myself. I would say to the young me something along the lines of: 'Man make the money, money never make the man. It's not about what you got, it's about your actions, your integrity along the way, like what you did to acquire the shiny things you've always wanted?'

Now the fact is that a roadman can purposely go blind when in the pursuit of getting money, power and respect. That same road-man-tality allows a man to risk his liberty and put his family's peace at jeopardy all for the sake of getting quick money or glory! Young me, can you honestly look in the mirror and tell yourself this represents a good standard of manhood to you? I mean, would you like to have grown up with a father in and out of jail? Or worse, have the actions of your father come to your home?'

The younger me: 'Of course not, but it is what it is.'

The older me: 'No, brother, it is what we make of it. And a real man knows he can't be a real man to his family from a jail cell.' I would probably leave the conversation there and leave him to figure it out on his own. However, I wouldn't judge the younger me for having that mindset because I totally get how we mislearn this idea of manhood. Especially without a positive father figure present. I now believe that a person who describes themselves as a roadman is actually a Prisoner to the Streets. So let's break down what a Prisoner to the Streets is further.

My 'Prisoner to the Streets' theory has four stages.

Stage 1: A Child's Innocence Before the Prisoner – this is about learned behaviours. They say children are like sponges soaking up all the information around them. Well, I agree, and a lot of boys I grew up with became Prisoner to the Streets, partly because we didn't have the tools to deal with things such as fear, conflict resolution, emotional maturity, childhood trauma, embarrassment, as well as a range of other things. This stage is all about the child before the change.

Stage 2.1: The Unconscious Prisoner – this stage looks at how young men/boys have learned certain behaviours and how those individuals have practised those learned behaviours so much that they have unconsciously become a Prisoner to the Streets. They begin to normalise those behaviours. It's at this stage where we begin to mislearn manhood. We unconsciously learn misguided pride, misguided loyalty, identity issues, peer pressure, self-pressure and so on.

Then we have *Stage 2.2: The Conscious Prisoner* – the stage where the Prisoner to the Streets has realised that the roadman mentality has got him trapped in a life of violence and/or crime. In this stage, he acknowledges that he has very little to no real peace of mind. However, although he has now become aware that a ride-or-die mentality brings with it a lot of drama, he refuses to change it. He is now aware the life he lives is self-destructive. He now realises it could end in murder or life in prison, but this doesn't stop the Conscious Prisoner from living by these roadman values. The Prisoner to the Streets is now conscious of being a roadman trapped in the cycle, but still won't leave it behind. Why? For two main reasons – fear and 'principles'. Fear of how others around him in that mindset might perceive him to be. And principles because although he has now become aware that he is a prisoner, he still identifies himself with this mindset and believes that the choices he has to make going forward as a roadman are just a case of survival. The streets have become his identity, who is he without road.

Some Prisoners to the Streets are so set in their way of thinking that they honour the man who lives a self-destructive path over the man who fights for a constructive one. For example, some roadmen see the man working a 9–5 as weak. While the man who goes to jail for trapping comes home to a circle praising him like he's just returned from some type of ghetto rite of passage.

The man who turns the other cheek is perceived as weak, while the man who kills over pride and ego is deemed as real. The man who is economically poorer because he won't go down a certain path as a result of his morals is perceived as inadequate, while the man who is economically rich but has no conscience is considered a real G (man).

The sad reality is that a young man who is becoming a Prisoner to the Streets views a roadman as the closest thing to what being a 'stand-up man' is. He buys into this so much that he strives towards it as a form of manhood. He patterns the behaviours down to a T, and ends up in some unfortunate positions like the roadmen before him. When I lived by the 'road mentality', I learned the hard way that it's impossible to be a 'stand-up man' in a world where a judge can tell me to sit down for years, over the man code I lived by.

Stage 3: Prisoner up for parole – this is the stage where the conscious prisoner is awoken. He now realises that the mindset he has doesn't accurately define manhood. Nor does it represent to him the best quality of life he could possibly be living. Now that he is awoken, the possibility that he can be freed from this 'Prisoner to the Streets' mindset has him feeling optimistic about the future. In a real-life situation, a Prisoner up for parole must prove he is a changed man before he is granted early release. The same kind of goes for a Prisoner to the Streets. Before a Prisoner to the Streets gets their freedom they have to prove they have changed the way they think. The only difference between the two prisoners up for parole is that the convicted prisoner can lie to the parole panel to get his freedom. While the Prisoner to the Streets can't cheat his way to freedom, he has to put the work in if he wants true freedom.

The PTTS has to rehabilitate himself to become free from the street prison. That man has to learn how better to deal with conflict resolution. He has to learn to become more responsible. That man has to dig deep for his purpose. He has to learn a new version of keeping it real. He has to let go of ego and learn to pride himself on doing good things, things which provide him with a better standard of living.

Stage 4: Final stage (Post–Traumatic Street Syndrome). This section is for those who are living with the after-effects of some of the things they witnessed or have done while living by the 'Prisoner to the Streets' mindset. And as a result, they need emotional healing to be able to function properly internally. But this is a subject matter within itself for another essay.

So now we know what a Prisoner to the Streets is, who is most likely to become one? I suppose in some cases it's hard to determine this. However, I believe those more vulnerable to becoming victims to this mentality are young people who experience a lot of trauma growing up. Or those who have experienced neglect and high levels of fear. Also those who are living in council flats or houses in areas with high crime rates and little to no stability at home. And not to forget those who are easily influenced or those that feed into peer pressure. There are so many contributing factors which make young people vulnerable to this mindset. Such as low self-esteem, no self-worth: these things alone can lead someone down a path of self-destructive behaviours.

On the flipside, though, believe it or not, you don't have to come from a council flat/area with high crime rate and a broken family to fall victim to this mentality. And this is why it can be hard to determine at times. Some Prisoners to the Streets come from good backgrounds. Good backgrounds in the sense where both parents live lovingly together in the same house. The crime rate is lower than Sesame Street and the community is one. That same child may have all the things he needs to get a head start in life, like a stable home, great education and great financial support. And still somehow fall victim to the street mentality. Why? Well, having the latest of everything and love at home isn't enough for him. Because that privileged young Prisoner now respects the roadman more than the man in his house who's provided for him all he needs. The privileged Prisoner somehow feels the need to act this way, as though he is looking for some form of acceptance from those who are lost with good reason. The privileged Prisoner may be a straight-A student, but dumb himself down just to be accepted. For me, it's always much harder to empathise with the person who chooses this 'road-mentality' over the young person who got caught up by negative surroundings and circumstance. In any case, a Prisoner to the Streets is a Prisoner to the Streets, so it's an issue that can't be ignored. It's an issue that supports the argument that this 'road-mentality' is also becoming fashionable to those who aren't as vulnerable as others. That somehow the pain of a few is being exploited through a sensationalist glamorisation of a roadman lifestyle, and all that leads to is more, not fewer, Prisoners to the Streets.

What are the solutions to stop young men being trapped in a Prisoner to the Streets mentality?

Well, growing up, I learned and became familiar with being told that my circle of people had a 'crabs in the bucket mentality'. I wouldn't argue it because it felt like there was some truth to it. What I didn't like about the statement was my intelligence being compared to a crab trapped in a bucket! I mean, surely if a group of humans *were* trapped in a 'crab mentality', we would have the sense to just get out of the bucket? No? I mean, after all, we are not crabs, we can communicate. Then it hit me that we *are* those crabs. And when it comes to solutions, we act like it is impossible to change things. They've given up hope so it's every crab for himself. But imagine if those crabs in the bucket stopped feeling defeated about being in the bucket and fought together to get out of it. Imagine they all use their crab claws, climb to the top and all manage to make the bucket tilt over. I know it sounds farfetched, but the reality is there is always a way.

But, like I said, we've become those crabs. So instead of figuring out a way to get out of the bucket, we invest our feelings and consume thoughts about who put us in the bucket. Or about who keeps throwing more injustices in the bucket and created the bucket for us. All the while pulling each other back. What I'm saying is the solution is internal. We need to know what the problem is before we can begin to fix it. So is the problem gun crime? Knife crime? No, these weapons might be used to solve people's problems, but they shouldn't be a focus. Why? Cos guns don't kill people, people kill people. The easy access to weapons is a massive problem, yes. But getting rid of the weapons won't necessarily get rid of the violence. Hence why the new evil-minded craze is acid. So the solution has to be to teach the young their worth and how to become men without turning to the streets.

The solution is and has always been about *prevention*. The solution is to educate a whole generation about the myths of the street, the myths of being a roadman. The solution is to get people to stop flippantly using the label 'gangs' and the narrative that goes with that and start looking at these young boys for whom they've unconsciously become, Prisoners to the Streets. Once you can do that, you will find you can empathise before passing a blanket judgement about this mentality which is wasting so many precious young lives.

The second part of the solution is *intervention*. Once again, I'm not talking about intervention from outside, an outside source we're waiting for to put things right for us. I'm talking about us, the crabs in the bucket, putting things right for ourselves. Some of the older roadmen from the community need to help out and admit this mentality isn't working for us. In fact it's killing us. We all need to be honest about the fears we really face. We need to all be men and set positive examples. Otherwise we become part of the problem and not part of the solution. Their truth is so valuable that it may be older roadmen who can actually set these young boys free from the streets. If as older roadmen, as individuals, we don't choose to have a conscience and help out our young brothers, then sadly we are making a decision to leave those crabs to figure it out on their own, instead of helping them to work together to tip the bucket over.

The primary aim has to be to focus on the younger genera-tions. Leave the older crabs to keep pulling each other back if after trying we can't get through. That might sound harsh but there's an old Caribbean saying: 'Those who don't hear must feel', and we can't waste energy on trying to get people to change if they are stuck in their ways.

Another focus area of intervention is effective parenting. Many parents feel restricted in the way they can parent their children due to legalities. In other words, are scared to smack their children. Now I'm not saying we should smack our children and I'm not saying we shouldn't. What I'm saying is we need to set boundaries and discipline from a young age. Then we need to be consistent with our methods of discipline. And we need to explain while disciplining our children what we are protecting them from. And that it comes from a place of love. We can't be holding back from teaching our children right from wrong because maybe we found our parents were too strict on us growing up. We don't have time for all that, we are in a time where our children are going astray and we can't afford to be there, bredrins. But yes, we must also *listen* and talk to our children more. Tell them we love them more. Educate them, empower them. We must have a positive open honest relationship with our children to allow them to grow wise and learn life. Broken families (couples) need to be fixed enough to work together for the sake of the child who needs love. Parenting isn't to blame for the problems we have, but good parenting can go a long way to helping solve them.

There are so many other things we can do to help solve this, but I feel the objectives would be much better met if us crabs in the bucket lived in togetherness. That way, we could build our own businesses and have our own schools and colleges teaching Black history, economics, culture, etc. That way, maybe we wouldn't even have to be quick to leave the bucket, maybe we could build upon it instead?

Yes, it's true that I never chose to be an author but that the pen chose me, and I definitely didn't grow up a reader. In fact, there was a time just after the publication of my debut novel, *Mama Can't Raise No Man*, when I had written more books than I had read. But when I wrote my memoir, I began an unconscious journey which was bigger than books. It's a journey I now consciously embrace. A journey which I hope results in saving lives. My weapons of choice to fight this mental war our young people are facing? Words, ideas and books.

'Optimism is the faith that leads to achievement. Nothing can be done without hope and confidence.' – Helen Keller.

Troubles With God

Okechukwu Nzelu

'Are you here for the service?'

I nod.

He looks at me, his eyes darting to my clothes. 'It's an hour.'

I nod again, undeterred.

He nods, the same way the guy who fixed my bike nods when I brought my muddy, broken old bike into his shop: grimly, and with the urge to get out of the hose. *All right then, if you're sure . . .*

'Come with me,' he says.

The small, elderly man leads me round the pews at the front to where the congregants are seated, waiting for Evensong in the chapel. Somehow, he is wearing a suit, despite the sweltering weather. I am inappropriately – scandalously, really – attired in a T-shirt and a pair of pink shorts that, not reaching my knees, whisper faintly of youth and a kind of wilfully insouciant sense of camp. I sense that both may be equally out of place in a church.

And yet, frustratingly, this outfit is the product of more than a few minutes' deliberation over the course of the week. What, after all, does one wear, to meet God? Should I have worn my most expensive clothes? Should I have covered my knees and elbows or does He make allowances for unusually sunny days? I was out in the sunshine with my friends all day – should I have gone home and changed? Is it important that I haven't seen Him in a long time? Should I have dressed up?

As I shuffle past members of the congregation (all over the age of about fifty, almost all white), they are all definitely thinking that I should have worn trousers. *Where did he think he was going to be?* they muse. *Canal Street?*

Eyes lowered (it's the only modesty I have to hand), I take a seat between a woman in running gear and two men in pinstripe suits and pocket squares. At least it's not just me.

It's just us, in here.

There are about twenty of us in here and I don't believe in God – but I think that could be a good thing. Sometimes, time away allows you to clarify your thoughts, to get some perspective. I have had plenty of time to think about religion and the thing I have realised about it is this: no matter how much you build it up or strip it down, there is probably nothing on earth more *human* than faith. Whatever the lofty labels people ascribe to their motivations, the things people do to one another in the name of religious belief – unbelievably kind, unforgivably cruel – are all so deeply human, so closely connected to the things that make us what we are. This, surely, is partly why I am here. Yes, I love the music, the meditative calm, but there is also the pull towards what is human, too.

Besides, I'm sure they wouldn't know I don't believe. I've been coming to church, one way or another, since I was a small child: first with my family, then in the choir at university and then, every now and then, at moments like this, when I feel something between need and desire. I know the routines: when to stand, when to kneel, when it's OK to sit even though some people choose to kneel; when to sing, when to speak, when to be silent. I respect and understand it, although I do not to believe in the God behind it. Despite my shorts, I fit in here.

And, truth be told, I feel a mixture of comfort and guilt about that. Growing up, I never went to the kind of churches that many of my Black friends went to: the kind where spontaneity was allowed (as at a Quaker Meeting I went to with a friend) and the presence of young people was routinely acknowledged. And the last choir I sang in formally was a chapel choir at Cambridge: two services a week, gowns, processions . . . An old fear stirs as it occurs to me that my experience of this thing that's so universally human has been very particularly *white*.

But I stop myself there: that kind of thinking can land you in hot water. I once read that Langston Hughes, on his first visit to Africa, threw some books over the side of the ship for fear that he would not be seen as authentically Black when he arrived[1]. What does it mean when a Black man throws his books overboard? What does it mean when a white man sees a Black man walk into a church wearing pink shorts and wonder why he's there?

I look around to see if the hymn numbers are displayed; they are not. What am I here for, anyway? It's hard to say. It's a funny thing for me to do, really, coming to church. It's a little bit like conducting a clandestine romantic affair: God and I parted ways a few years ago now – for very good reasons – it's been years since we saw each other regularly, and only my closest friends know that I'm seeing Him again. What would people think?

But, then, was it any easier to say why I went to church, even when I did believe in God? Or why I kept going for weeks, even after I felt myself losing my faith? When I was a child, I took most things seriously – myself, my school work, reading the novel before watching the film, reading novels right up until the end even if they were bad, reading the instruction manual,

---

1 Chinitz, David E. *Which Sin to Bear? Authenticity and Compromise in Langston Hughes* (Oxford: Oxford University Press, 2013)

reading the fine print in the instruction manual, trying to read the French-language page of the instruction manual – but especially God. Until I was about seventeen, I believed very strongly that there was a God in Heaven looking down on us, quietly ordering the world and ensuring that even the most seemingly tragic of events were all part of a greater plan for the world's good. At one point, I prayed before bed and before meals. I read the Bible *in my spare time*.

Thinking back on that, now, I wonder how I must have come across to non-believers. Even rereading that paragraph to myself, it seems odd. How could I have lived like that? How could I have thought about the world like that?

Those who have a strong religious faith are often perceived as at least a little bit odd. Surely only the desperate, the privileged or the wilfully blind can look at the world as it truly is, and see a benevolent God anywhere near it? I speak from experience: since I stopped believing myself I have had more than one conversation with someone who seemed 'normal' but turned out to believe that, for example, God created women to be subservient to men, or that gay people deserve to go to hell, along with their shorts. It's unnerving.

But I never was that kind of Christian, and, as the organist plays, I hazard a guess that the people around me aren't either. We're garden-variety Anglicans, here: we sit at the back, we don't make much noise, we keep ourselves to ourselves, we try to cover our knees in church but we don't make a fuss if it's a really hot day and someone just couldn't help it. We're Not That Kind of Christian.

I found (and still find) fundamentalist, intolerant faith frustrating, in part because it seems impossible – it seems more like certainty, which is easy, than faith, which is much harder – and it made genuine faith like mine (difficult, troubling, real) harder to share in public, for fear of reprisal or judgement. Many people – especially among my atheist white-English friends, for some of whom religion is no longer much of a cultural phenomenon so much as a sort of sideshow oddity – greet people of deep religious faith with a mixture of indulgence and polite wariness. I suppose that's how some people must have thought of a younger me.

And yet, sitting down to Evensong, I can't help but feel that this is an unfair assessment. Perhaps it's the magic of the liturgy, working its spell (the organist has been quietly playing for the past ten minutes, the choir enters in their purple cassocks and I run my fingers over the leather of *The New English Hymnal*), but slowly, slowly I feel myself slipping back into the habit of – not faith, no, but something close to it; its embrace, its smell, its robes. There are some people who have never believed in a god or gods, and who cannot imagine what it feels like to be loved by one; I am not one of those people and I am grateful for it this evening. All of the trappings of faith are familiar to me, like the smell of an auntie's shampoo when you hug. It feels like being welcomed back into a family I haven't seen for years, a family I had forgotten was mine.

Growing up, religion was just part of life. I've never really understood why even the most fervent religious belief requires people to have to get up early on a Sunday – or why the universe seemed to conspire to make us late for church without fail – but get up we did, and late we were. The churches we went to were friendly ones, and although I rarely met people my age there and almost never socialised with anyone in the congregation, I remember feeling welcomed. It felt like a kind of community, in a way, and it saddens me that there are hardly any other real ways in which that concept exists in England, today.

And within that community, I developed my own faith. I believed that God was watching us closely, but that he, surely, had better things to do than watch, askance, as men held hands.

I remember going to Nigeria for the first time, as a young

child, and being taken to a church service (again, late) which was entirely spoken in Igbo. Like a growing number of young Igbos, I've never become fluent, so attending the service was like feeling my way around a familiar house at night with the lights off: I knew the direction in which I was heading, and I recognised the vague shape of things, but the specifics evaded me, things appearing out of nowhere that I had never seen in the half-light, never noticed, not known well enough to look for in a different context. I recognised the patterns, but not the words.

Yet, despite my ignorance, religion felt familiar, on that visit to Nigeria. It felt strong. It was everywhere: a relative told me that mosques and churches were being built faster than they could get people to worship in them. At another relative's house, we had prayers every morning, followed by a lesson on a passage from the Bible. It felt like home.

In the church, the choir sings: *My soul doth magnify the Lord, and my spirit hath rejoiced in God my saviour . . .*

But things were not always easy. Back in England, as a child, I remember seeing a magazine lying around the house. It was a sort of newsletter with information about developments and achievements of people 'back home'. On its glossy pages were grainy photographs of smiling people, young and old, graduands, grandparents, newlyweds. Flicking through it, I came across an article that sticks in my mind to this day: 'Turning Our Men into Their Women'. I frowned and examined the article further.

As I read on, its logic became clear: the writer, like many others before and after him, claimed that homosexuality was a Western import. More than this, the title seemed to claim that the very nature of homosexuality itself was not merely foreign to Africa, but traitorous, an act of treachery. Presumably, this was an Africa in which neither knowledge nor pink shorts are welcome.

But this kind of argument is something I'm familiar with. Partly because a lot of African history was preserved orally until colonialism began in earnest around the turn of the nineteenth century, partly because England does not sufficiently educate itself about the true nature of Empire, and partly because there are people and organisations with a vested interest in misremembering the truth, it is a common misconception that homosexuality did not exist in Africa until Westerners arrived and gave people All Sorts of Ideas. As historians and journalists have since pointed out – including Bisi Alimi, in his article for the *Guardian* on 9 September 2015[2] – this was simply not the case. The missionaries who, in Nigeria, worked closely with more overtly aggressive colonial powers to venture further into what would become part of the Commonwealth, brought homophobia with them in massive quantities, the same way that smallpox was being imported halfway across the world.

Earlier this year, I was surprised to learn that Theresa May had issued something resembling an apology for one of the British Empire's less fashionable exports, the anti-homosexuality laws which are now pervasive across the Commonwealth. I think a lot of people probably know that the British Empire wasn't all fun and games, but I suspect most people don't know the true extent of the damage it did in many ways, this being one of them, and I wonder how many people heard May's statement, Googled *anti-homophobic laws in Commonwealth*, and looked at Black people slightly differently.

I was surprised to hear May's statement of regret. I am disappointed (but not surprised) that representatives from the Church did not join with her in a similar statement. As Alimi reminds us

2 'If you say being gay is not African, you don't know your history', Bisi Alimi, *Guardian*, 5 September 2015, https://www.theguardian.com/commentisfree/2015/sep/09/being-gay-african-history-homosexuality-christianity

in his article, the answer is transparency, openness and education. The absence of these things creates the kind of ignorance in which bigotry and hatred thrive and spread.

Lord, now lettest Thou Thy servant depart in peace . . .

The troubling presence of absolute certainty and blissful ignorance were, ultimately, behind my decision to leave the Church when I was seventeen. Although my reasoning has developed since then, and grown more complex, I simply could not understand how a loving God could allow His words to be misinterpreted to the detriment of so many of His children. Wouldn't He – shouldn't He – have made Himself more clear? Wouldn't He have done . . . something? How could He let so many people suffer and die in His name?

The Problem of Evil (that is, the apparent contradiction between the level of unnecessary, fruitless suffering in the world and the idea of a loving, all-powerful God) is a difficult one, and when I speak about it to people who have faith, most simply nod and smile wearily, admitting that it is something they struggle with, too. Even as a child I was all-or-nothing, and I couldn't continue the struggle: it was too painful, too difficult; it didn't seem authentic any more to defend a God who presided over a world in which hate can pile upon hate. I couldn't believe in a God like that, and I still can't.

The music stops. The spell is broken. The choir processes out and, after a few contemplative moments, I walk out into the sunshine.

And yet I know I will be back. I always come back. I cannot ignore the things about religion that I find troubling – its ripeness for abuse, its close links to some of the very worst parts of culture and human nature. But nor can I ignore the things about it that I deeply, deeply love: the urge to forgive past wrongs; the call to a struggle towards bettering oneself, to meet impossibly high expectations of character and of the human heart; even the music. I will probably never believe again, but I will be back. And, if it's warm enough, so will my shorts, because, ultimately, the God I really believe in still exists.

Imagine if there were a being who'd seen you at your most proud and your most vulnerable; someone who knows you deeply and is unafraid of that knowledge. Someone who knows that you can sometimes be petty and lazy, as well as generous and thoughtful; who thinks that all the different things about you that other people find anomalous or threatening or unknowable are actually pretty great. That's the God I want. It's the God I fell in love with as a teenager. It's the God I prayed to at the darkest moments in my life, and the God I thanked and praised when I survived them. It's the God I believe in and – not to get all weekly column about it, but of course, of course, of course, all that time, he was really just the best version of myself, challenging me to be the best I can, to be forgiving, to build, to connect, to understand, to sustain, to support, to give, always insisting that even at my worst I'm still enough.

He's who I'm here to see. I have come here, I know now, to remind myself that He still exists, always has. It's not often I'm in church these days, perhaps because I learned to look out for Him in the everyday. And in the moments (more frequent as I get older) when I recognise Him in myself and others, I still – as, I think, should you – rejoice.

Black Greatness

Stephen Morrison-Burke

As in life, there are times when a fighter is losing a battle, when no matter how much he tries he can't seem to find his rhythm or break that of his oppressor. During a sustained attack, the fighter may be subjected to relentless physical and psychological abuse, which, coupled with his exhaustion and exasperation, may slowly cause him to lose all concern for not only the fight itself, but also for his general wellbeing. Negative thoughts will regurgitate in these tough times, thoughts of inferiority, reiterated by the masses.

Towards the end of the first round, my opponent was in the middle of such an attack when he span off to the right and threw a looping right hook, catching me flush on the point of the chin. I had no recollection between the punch landing and me realising I was sat on the seat of my shorts with the referee standing over me.

'... TWO ... THREE ... FOUR ...' he shouted, the fingers on his right hand flicking up by the second.

The crowd were estatic. Only in a football stadium with the home team having just scored had I heard anything like the explosion of joy in that working-men's club when I found myself on the canvas. The familiar feeling of not being enough, of having never been enough, kept me stationary. I thought of those I was letting down, including family members at home who'd told me they had every faith I'd win; thought of my coach over in my corner; of the young kids back at the gym who looked up to me, the ones who would inevitably gather round me at the beginning of Monday's training session to ask if I'd won, and I relived the despondency in their eyes the last time I said, 'No. I lost.'

And yet, whilst sat in a vortex of my own negative emotions, something extraordinary happened. I lost all fear of losing. I didn't want to lose, but the knockdown had somehow eradicated the fear of falling short of victory. Up was the only way for me to go now. A gust of new life had come to me at the precise moment I was preparing to accept defeat. It felt as though some force larger than myself, a reserve of energy I couldn't possibly have accounted for, was imploring me to rise and give my all to the battle. Right there, down on that blood-soaked canvas, the fight took on a new purpose for me. It was no longer about a decision adjudicated by three indifferent judges, but about how much of myself I'm willing to sacrifice for what I believe in.

There were very few Black people involved in the sport of boxing at the time I made my slow walk towards the ring on that November night in Southampton. I rarely took friends and family to watch me, but didn't much mind the feeling of isolation, for I was familiar with being stared at, sneered, and sometimes jeered at, as all men of colour are. Boxing had become a reflection of my day-to-day life, therefore I felt well equipped to deal with whatever it threw my way. I passed through the middle of the hostile crowd and climbed through the ropes into the ring to be confronted by the referee who asked to see my gumshield, checked my gloves for defects, and knocked on the protector under my shorts with the back of his hand to ensure I was wearing one. He then walked across to the opposite corner of the ring and went through the same process with my opponent.

After the MC had introduced us by our surnames and the colours of our corners – cheers for my opponent, boos for me – the referee called us both to ring centre where we stood almost nose to nose.

'Let's have a good, clean fight, boys,' said the ref. 'I want you to stop at my command, and when I say "break" I want you to step back. Best of luck to you both. Now touch gloves and return to your corners.'

In those few seconds of staring at my adversary, I was able to answer all the questions that had plagued my mind in the run-up to the fight. Has he trained as hard as me? Is he as hungry for victory as I am? Does he know pain, true pain? Is life a continual uphill struggle for him, too? I felt I was able to see into my opponent's soul and was happy for him to see into mine, to learn there were no discrepancies between the revelations in my eyes and the fight I would bring to him. I always knew from those few seconds of eye contact whether a contest would be a tough one or not, irrespective of whose hand was raised after the final bell.

The time-keeper then rang the bell to begin the first round and we danced, light feet, gloves up, chins tucked to chest. Men with pint glasses in their hands shouted expletives interwoven into instructions they'd never carried out themselves. A handful of women screamed from the pit of their lungs, much of it indecipherable to me. Occasionally, I'd hear the words 'Kill him!' and glance over to see a contorted countenance beetroot with fury, eyes glaring my way, as we unleashed quick combinations in one another's direction. Adults and children gradually worked their excitement up towards a frenzy, all gratified in the name of entertainment. That's when I got knocked down.

'FIVE... SIX... SEVEN,' the referee continued.

By the time he'd reached eight I was stood facing him, my opponent across the ring in a neutral corner banging his gloves together with a greater sense of confidence.

With the flame in the fighter's spirit now reignited, the body he can't feel much of begins to propel him forward. He's not entirely sure how, but on he pushes. If the fighter's opponent has never suffered the indignity of taking a beating himself, has never been down and endured the humiliation that comes with it, he can neither fully comprehend, replicate, nor prevent the spiritual resurgence of a man determined to rise from the brink of defeat. With gritted teeth, the fighter who had to climb from the canvas now sees a flicker of light in front of him. He finds hope.

There's a major shift in energy. The opponent, clearly ahead on the scorecards, will try to nullify this fightback, but the momentum has now passed from the attacker to his victim. The wounded fighter starts to find his own rhythm, his own sense of self, and no longer dances to the beat of his oppressor, who watches a flickering flame transform into a forest fire and inevitably curses himself for failing to extinguish the spirit of the wounded fighter when he had the chance.

Now that momentum has shifted in favour of the oppressed, his oppressor – the negator of Black greatness – must be held accountable. He is now subject to the wrath of all he attempted to suppress. With hands held high, the opponent attempts to protect and preserve his own wellbeing by boxing on the back foot to maintain the status quo. He might even begin to throw 'don't hit me punches', which is when a fighter doesn't fully commit to his attacks, acts half-heartedly in the hope his actions will be recip-rocated and his opponent will refrain from seeking a knockout.

This is when the fighter who had previously been subjected to a beating sees the wizard's clumpy shoes beneath the curtain, when he recognises his attacker and the now quietening crowd for who they truly are, all they ever were – mere mortals with an inflated sense of entitlement. The true measure of a man should not be taken when things are going well for him but when his back is against the ropes, when he's forced to face the same treatment he was happy to dish out. Some of the worst despots to ever live ruled with an air of indestructability, and yet ran and hid when their dictatorship met its downfall.

Greatness: notable; remarkable; exceptionally outstanding.
To be the very best version of yourself.

Black greatness is the biggest threat to institutional racism there is. It's an anathema to those who close doors in the faces of a rising people, often with an apology in public and a smirk in private. The individuals who consciously keep these discriminatory systems in place are never going to willingly step aside and allow the Black man to be great without a fight of some sort. And this is the important part, the trick: those pulling the strings of discrimination will claim that it isn't a fight and that to adopt such confrontational language is both extreme and incendiary and blows the current state of race relations in Britain out of all rational proportion. 'Why are you so angry? Calm down. Can't we all just get along peacefully...?' The anger is justified. The focus must now be for the Black man to sublimate that energy into his higher calling. He may not have written the unequal rules of modern-day combat, but he better understands the territory on which these rules are played out than those who did. He had to, to survive.

The suffering endured by the Black man and his forefathers has forced him to not only be incredibly resilient, but also extraordinarily creative. It's forced him to be resourceful when handed limited resources from which to draw from. Not so long ago I saw a video clip of a young Black boy on a London estate rapping to a beat from the phone in his hand whilst doing the *prisiadka*, the Slavic dance which involves squatting a few inches from the ground and alternating front kicks with both legs. Both laces on his white trainers were loose, a set of locked metal gates behind him. I watched it several times over and wanted to see more. Those who appropriate Black culture for financial gain feel the same way.

If Black British men can have such an incredible cultural influence on the language we use in this country, the music we listen to, the food we eat, and the clothes we wear, then it's fair to assume that when determined, disciplined and strong in faith, they can, without question, achieve dreams of monumental proportions. If Black men can continue to demonstrate the resilience required to sing and dance in both good and bad times, can recognise the true value of their innate fortitude, creativity and remarkable history, all whilst living in a world that continues to lean away from their wants and needs, there is no limit to what can be accomplished. I'll say it again in case you missed it. If disciplined, dedicated to his cause, and strong in faith – and these are big ifs in these times of increasing moral decadence – the Black British male is primed to achieve greatness.

People often ask me why, after however many rounds of punching each other in the face, do boxers embrace at the end of a contest. The answer is respect. A fighter who attempted to remove you from consciousness will hug you tighter than a loving parent when he learns that you will fight to the death for what you believe in. My personal belief is that the closest any two human beings can possibly be to one another is having fought either against each other, or together for a common cause. They may not like one another, but the two fighters have developed a spiritual connection, for better or for worse, that can't be delineated. No one has a greater understanding of the mercurial tendencies of the oppressor than the oppressed, not even himself.

At the end of the contest, and having fought hard after being knockdown, the referee congratulated me and my opponent on a 'cracking fight.' The same audience members that had screamed for my blood were now giving me a standing ovation, many of them quick to pat me on the back and share a kind word or two when I stepped from the ring. I'd shown them something. I'd shown them that the only beat I'm willing to dance to, in the ring as in life itself, is my own. I'd shown them that my self-worth is far greater than what they feel my definition of it should be. There was nothing I ever felt I had to prove to them – I boxed for personal reasons – but they had learned to acknowledge the heart of a fighter, a fighter of whom they may have regarded as inferior, and secretly feared, when they first laid eyes on me. But there were no shortcuts to harmony. The fight had to take place before respect was shown.

If Black men in this country are willing to aim for greatness, regardless of their chosen field of endeavour, they can do so with the reassurance that even if they fall short they'll still be among the gods. They'll be held aloft in the minds and hearts of millions of young Black children who will be encouraged to walk tall with the belief they too can someday float amid the ether of their wildest dreams.

I understand that for many people the talk of greatness will appear irresponsible balderdash, a fantasy that does well to avoid the practicalities of 'real life'. This is the mindset Black men must first free themselves from, and then, when in a more advantageous position, must reach back to free those same critics from. A mindset none of us entered this world with. The Black man must be continually seeking to lift his brothers and sisters to higher ground, to an elevated understanding of their own excellence, even if they are unaware higher ground exists.

Never before in this country has there been a better opportunity to raise a subjugated people back to the dizzy heights where it belongs than right now, in these times of socio-political disarray. The earth is now fertile for the Black man to rise and bring to light the divine brilliance that has been planted within him. He can move forward knowing the path before him has already been cleared. His own gratuitous suffering and that endured by his ancestors is his right of passage, has created a positive karma he is owed and must now be willing to not only collect, but truly believe he, those around him and those that have gone before him fully deserve.

Three days after my boxing match, a homeless man, sat crossed-legged against a brick wall outside Putney Bridge Station in London, called out to me and a friend. I'd just given him a handful of new books and my friend had given him a pocket full of change. We walked back over to him, his dark clothes worn to threads in random places, his skin paler than the clouds he sat beneath.

'Can I ask you something?' he said.

'Yes, mate, go ahead,' I replied.

'Why is it mostly Black people that stop to help me?'

Me and this homeless man stared at each other long enough for me to realise his question wasn't a rhetorical one. I spoke in a tone loud enough for only the three of us to hear when I said, 'Because we know what it's like to be down.'

Where Do Black Men Go to Dance?

Symeon Brown

On Fridays the queues into 588a Kingsland Road were a catwalk of luxury streetwear. You could spot the Fashion Nova freakum dress or the two-piece Supreme tracksuit. In the queue were the white girls wearing fitted jeans with Stan Smiths and the Black boys in throwback Ellesse. In contrast to the West End's sterile dress policies, the fitted cap and trainers were uniform – and although there wasn't anything that you couldn't wear, there were certainly things that every aspiring east London cool kid tried to. In the crowd of Blair's babies just arriving at their adult years, I was one of Thatcher's grown-ass kids in the overdraft of my extended adolescence. I'm a big man, but I'm not thirty, so here I came, trying to get into the club that my mother used to rave at in the mid-90s that now played music by the emcees who I grew up beside.

I was born in Hackney in east London where Visions Video Bar has resided on Kingsland Road for a quarter of a century. I came of age in Tottenham, if you follow the Kingsland Road north for another fifteen minutes. Like the surrounding area, the club found a fashionability as a purposely unglamorous basement sweatbox, playing the music working-class Black people make and dance to. I have only known Visions to be steaming and one of the few places to weekly play the music I like to bruk out to. The club rose to a wave of popularity following a downturn in the mid- to late-2000s that sparked a rethink by the club's founder.

The 2000s were an awful time to be a Black British schoolboy in London, at least for me. Our entire culture – from the music to our hoodies – was a coping mechanism long before it became the must-have commodity it is today. I don't know anyone who did not have a tag name and a sixteen-bar introduction on who you wanted others to believe you were. In my friendship group we had a Mighty Mo and a Maestro. In the year above, there was a Black the Ripper. Now just known as Black.

In school playgrounds, and on street corners across the ends, barely pubescent boys like me found different ways to say we refused to be emasculated over arcade-inspired 140-BPM riddims programmed into a Nokia handset. For me, these events were a cathartic release of fear disguised in boundless energy and aggression. Mini mosh pits were like an exorcism. Dancing was how I felt most free, but others found liberation on the microphone. Some, like Black, turned out to have a gift for it and, for them, our culture became a craft. The most organised in my area took to Heat and AXE FM and found hood fame, but then, not much fortune. That would all change.

The backdrop to this was warfare. Knife fights at youth hubs. Gunshots in nightclubs. Violence was en vogue and boys starting to squad up. Nights out meant rolling twenty to fifty man deep if you were lucky and if you were not, you could end up a victim of eaters, or worse. A friend and I were held up and robbed on a bus and after the police asked us to do our own policing, my friend's response was to buy a crossbow off of eBay that arrived within a few weeks. Youth violence was a city-wide public health epidemic and now it had a soundtrack too.

I don't remember when they started calling it Grime but I do recall when the police said it was dangerous, just like they proclaim today about UK drill. It's 2018 but the police have deployed the same moral panic and tactics that closed down Black club nights where Black men and women liked to dance. This was before a young ambitious promoter named Gianno rocked up in the basement of 588 Kingsland Road where he encountered the man known as Eddy Visions.

Eddy Augustine is the man who gave Visions Video Bar life in 1989 and, almost thirty years later, he relayed the club's genesis to me in that very basement.

'It was me and my late partner Wayne Yarde who first put Visions together but originally we started as a sound system in the early 80s and then we developed into a big professional system that allowed us to play out all over the country.'

Music and performance run through Eddy's veins. He has a wide smile that gates a soft Grenadan accent that was once heard tearing up the mic as a formidable emcee, while his late partner spun the tracks.

'Wayne was a soul man. He could select [songs] that would mash up the dance. Me, I was [into] reggae, soca and calypso. I was the one on the microphone. I would get the people going and make the people feel comfortable and make them enjoy themselves and if I have to go on the dancefloor and dance for them and go on bad then I will do it. I will never like to know that someone come in my party and my dance and say they can dance better than me and I used to do all kinds of crazy things to win.'

It was this spirit that the man from west London's 1960s Caribbean community brought east. West London has been an incubator of British African–Caribbean culture while also retaining a tradition of hostility towards Black ravers. My sole experience of that was a short-lived night out when I was twenty, where the bouncers of a shoddy club informed me I did not fit the criteria and set me on my way to a two-hour commute back home on the night bus. It remains my first and last time begging for their acceptance. For Eddy, that same tradition prevented him from finding a venue closer to home decades earlier.

'We tried. West London was a bit more stush and it was more difficult, but east London had all the [Black] clubs, so it was easier for us to find a venue. They were more accepting, so we found this venue,' said Eddy.

However even east London was not devoid of discrimination. The agents acting on behalf of their landlord had even refused to do business with the Black entrepreneur, claimed Eddy.

'To get the lease for this property, I had to actually pretend to be somebody else. I used to work for BT and had a friend who was a white guy and we saw the lease in one of the estate agents around the corner from here. I walked in there and got blanked and so I got my white friend to come along with me. Basically he had a briefcase and they spoke to him and he was able to get the information. I've [now] been here thirty years. The first lease was for five years but it's a renewable lease.'

When Eddy first opened its doors, Visions Video Bar was a banqueting venue that invited promoters to put on the reggae and soul revival dances that lured revellers like my mother, while also catering for weddings, birthdays and funerals. Eddy described the aesthetic as posh and speaks with pride about his tiled rooms that had lots of mirrors and which were adorned with twenty-one then top-of-the-range Sony Trinitron screens for the video production and screening package they'd offer to wedding functions. There are eight left as a background aesthetic, but the club, for most of the past five years, has looked bare and typically east London, following Gianno's intervention to revive the club's fortunes because Eddy worried for its future.

'Gianno said "Well, you have to do this you have to do that."
[I said] "I'm not going to take my photographs down, my tiles
off the floor!" All the clubs in the area that started up had this
rough look, they took all the plaster off the wall.

'This place was beautiful and they [Gianno] gutted the place
but that was the look that the people wanted and Gianno came
and tore the look out of Visions and I never got over that. I'm
still traumatised.' He laughs but he gave Gianno the licence to
reinvent Visions in the way he saw fit.

You have to move with what's happening in the area. You
don't want to get left behind and in Gianno, Eddy found the
man to do it.

'He is very upbeat and very hungry. He is going somewhere,
you know what I mean. He's on the move.' Gianno's friends
describe him as having multiple phone numbers and the thirty-
something-year-old man is one of the most influential stealth
figures in London's party scene.

In the mid-20-teens, Gianno did not just bring a new aesthetic
but a new crowd. The nights were hosted by Boya Dee, hood
famous for being an emcee in the cult group NU Brand Flexx.
The grim aesthetic of Visions seemed to suit the recognised
faces of the Grime scene who still remembered being cast out of
the West End. Visions was very casual, rough and provided the
easy weekend home for Skepta and Boy Better Know, as they
rode an upward wave during Grime's resurgence, thanks to the
Internet's ability to subvert the infamous 696 form.

The Internet democratised the ability of artists to reach mass
markets and broke the distribution cartel. The boys who were
doing music as culture now had a borderless industry in their
own hands and no shortage of suitors. Online their music was
growing and offline Visions was their weekend home.

After an initially frosty first meeting, Gianno invited a DJ
named Joel to play regularly on Fridays and Saturdays. Several

years on and Joel succeeded the promoter as events manager of the club. He's been a regular fixture of the club's ascent.

'At that time Grime was in a resurgence and was incredibly credible,' said Joel. 'Now Grime is established, it's a part of British heritage.' Visions was the place to be.

'Boya on stage tearing it up and BBK taking the mic off him and the mic going round and everyone going nuts.

'We used to call it school and the youth club because this is where we used to come to see our friends and that's what it is and this is where Black people come to assert what it is to be Black and British.'

However this comes with caveats because it was here Visions' clientele began to shift somewhat. Boya notes how the popularity of the Grime scene began to draw in a crowd of celeb watchers. Drake, A$AP Rocky and Pharrell Williams would be some of the A-listers who would all pass through.

Visions introduced an exclusive guest list policy with a team who screened Facebook requests to get onto the list, not just by gender and good looks like most clubs but also by the patronage of Visions's core inner circle of artists, entourages and Gianno himself. Even Joel concedes in the early days that he could not get in.

'[It's] because I wasn't friends with Gianno. I thought I could get in here and I rocked up and I couldn't. I really had no intention of weaseling my way in. I was like that's what it was. All people have to do is reach out to us, talk to the bar staff, the people on the door, talking to all kinds of people from different industries, they are invested in this place.'

There's a law of the playground in operation. Without access to the inner circle of cool, the door is closed. One Friday, a blind request from me was denied for myself and a friend visiting from the US, albeit via the discretion of my Facebook inbox rather than a humiliation at the door. Try again, it said, when you have more girls with you. London is so limited a city for spontaneity at night that there was nowhere else to go playing our music that was not ticketed. Most nights that are not require the old trick of befriending groups of girls for camouflage so the bouncer doesn't disperse my friends and me.

Visions was supposed to be the place where Black men can go to dance and it is where east London's hipsters converge with the creatives of the hood, but like the West End club it's meant to be an antidote to, it appears to have a *de facto* quota on the number of Black men it allows in who aren't famous to the nation or the hood.

'There's some people who make it in and I see that they've never been here and they are local and I feel for them because I wouldn't want them to have that stigma that it was hard for them to get in. It's provided a traction for people who had to go to the West End and get turfed from clubs at the West End. Unfortunately that same process has happened in Hackney but as long as you send the names you will have a good time. I don't think it's that hard to access Visions. It's just about how much they want to.'

Despite this, Joel does not accept that the club's tighter rules and its growing popularity has had this impact.

'The guest list system forces people to take responsibility over their night. I just can't get on-board that that would alienate any regulars or locals.'

For Eddy, it ensured the safety of that night.

'I think the guest list for me is to try and filter out more the decent people for them to enjoy themselves. They could be Indian, Black, white, it doesn't matter. You won't get no problem. It takes just one person to upset a whole club.' He adds not everyone is 'desirable', if they are a threat to security.

Visions never really had the infrastructure to operate an exclusive tiering system like a Mayfair club. Until recently, there were not any tables and so there was not any table service. A boiler-room cupboard, the size of two toilet cubicles, and a podium in front of the DJ booth had been the closest thing to operating a VIP area. This tiny area within the club hosted the smattering of hood-famous Black men and members of their entourages, surrounded by a uniform of attractive young white women and the occasional ambiguous 'lightie.' To me, there was always a notable absence of dark-skin Black women to complement the plethora of dark-skin Black men.

In a society that reproduces the stories, importance and aesthetics of white Brits, anything created by anyone else is automatically counterculture, even if it was not intending to be. The artists that crammed into Vision's boiler room were the vanguard of our culture who stuck with it long enough for it to pay. The billion-pound media company VICE took it upon itself to make Grime their home and although appearing, on my visits at least, to have one of the least diverse newsrooms in journalism, pays for unparalleled access to the work of Black men. Skepta – the elder of Boy Boy Better Know, whose signature look was a black tracksuit – now has a high-end clothing line in uptown Selfridges. Gianno, who made his name at Visions club, has been sought to throw parties by corporate brands and private members' clubs like the Curtain and Soho House in need of exclusive parties.

Everybody wants in on this counterculture but where I come from that was just our common culture, so to be told on a Friday that the space won't let me in because the club's quota on Black men is over capacity not only left me with a sense of disownership, but also with the practical dilemma of where I could go to dance without a ticket.

Amid the popularity of Black music, there is no limit on the numbers of tracks by Black men that are played, but there is a limit on how many of us are let in to appreciate it. Black cool is a desirable product. Black people? Not so much. The West End club DSTRKT became infamous when two good-looking Black women were turned away because 'dark-skin Black girls had to be "extra hot"'. I have limited my personal experience of the West End's clubs simply because humiliation is not a feeling I enjoy.

Boya says when he and Gianno started running Visions, their plan was to recreate the romance of your 'first house party'. A plan that feels nostalgic because the London house party has been under threat from the cost of living here. The property boom has meant that the way young Londoners live has changed from prior generations. To be young in London on an average wage is to be first priced out of home-ownership and secondly out of being able to privately rent a decent place with a communal room, and social housing is a myth. In London, twenty-somethings new to the city live in shared houses with strangers and those born here opt to live with their families, if they can, to save money.

The cost of the city became a looming existential threat to Visions that went into the year 2018 as possibly Britain's longest-running Black-owned club.

'When we first started we all had promoters. All the clubs in this area, most of them had their events here. Passing Clouds [a now closed Bohemian venue around the corner], they had their functions down here. Voodoo Rays. As the Black clubs shut down, the white clubs opened up,' Eddy said.

'The lease running out is a problem and when it ends the rent goes up. The rent's gone up significantly. The rent's risen by 80% in the last ten years. The rent's risen a lot more in the last ten years than the last twenty because of what's happened. They want a lot more bars and quirky places to eat. The people who actually come to Dalston and live in Dalston has changed. It's like a storm. I saw it coming.'

Eddy may have seen the storm, but many of the young ravers who flooded into Visions were left stunned when it arrived in the form of a tweet. On 23 August 2018 at 9.01 p.m. the club tweeted, 'It is with a heavy heart that we must announce the immediate closure of the venue you know as Visions.'

The announcement was sudden. There was no final party. No warning. No anything. According to Joel, the club was put under pressure by its new neighbour – a block of luxury apartments for buyers with a spare million. If the new tenants here may have been charmed by Hackney's hipsterism, they were not prepared for its character of young ravers spilling out between 6 and 7 a.m. into their Ubers or onto the 149 bus. Joel said the club began to accrue complaints which threatened Eddy's thirty-year licence.

'Initially we cut our running hours down from 10 p.m. to 6 a.m. to closing at 4 a.m. but now, as the closure of other venues indicates, not even that could have saved us.'

Joel said Eddy took the decision to voluntarily close up to protect his licence and morph the club into something that might be more palatable to its neighbours. The problem is, that is unlikely to be me or, more accurately, us.

Visions's dance floor is now closed, and looking for another place to dance in this city is remarkably hard for a major capital. There is a greater demand than supply and most licences appear to run till just 2 a.m. This is the time when a good night in New York or Istanbul might start. Hackney even passed a ruling in 2018 that suggested new venues in Hackney had to close by midnight. The door policies of London clubs have felt to me far tighter than in cities like Manchester and the demand to get in always exceeds the capacity, so when clubs can pick and choose their clients, Black men appear to be their most undesirable consumers due to the expectation of violence attached. So where do we go to gully creeper? Where do we go to do the frog back, the shoki and to milly rock? Where do we go to make new connections and renew old ones?

The disappearance of public places to dance or even just to sit without the pressure of buying a coffee is often offset by the abundance of digital space. Instagram will give you an endless roll of tape and won't charge but a square metre in London can cost you up to £20,000 in some corners of the city. I congregate in digital spaces not only because it's convenient but also because it's free.

The Internet can occupy my mind, but it does nothing for my body. Nothing can replace the importance of dance. It's my body that lets me know I'm alive, which is why what I am able to do with mine on weekends matters more to me than my smartphone.

In the same way 140BPM sounds and bravado helped boys cope with fear in the mid-2000s, the release from a mosh pit or a slow whine helped me cope with the dull ache of living in a city that is slowly expelling me in 2017 in between my teens and thirties.

'If you look at it back in the day when we used to have the dances which your parents used to come to, the revival dances and that happened and then Visions become a nightclub and then you got the Joels and the Giannos and then now we are having it as a bar you can sit down and eat and have a few drinks but you have this area to sit down and we have this area you can dance. We are having a coffee machine in. It's still evolving,' says Eddy.

'Thousands of Black Londoners have their memories in the basement of this nightclub. I've had people who have got married here, and they've had their christening here and the child had their 18th and their 21st birthday party here and it's gone on.'

Venues like Visions matter not only as a site where Grime regained its confidence IRL, but because cities need places to dance. For me, it was where I could gun lean, shaku shaku, Azonto, heel and toe or learn whatever the new dance was.

Where do I go to dance now?

The Black Male Image ©
White People (til date)
Nels Abbey

'You've got to understand that you're dealing with the image of a fourteen-year-old child. And this child gonna be out there playing when your old ass and me gonna be in the grave. When she say something, we done told you what's happening. You're dealing with a little Black kid, and let her be a kid. She done answered it with a lot of confidence, leave that alone.'
– Richard Williams steps in to stop John McKenzie from damaging
  fourteen-year-old tennis player Venus Williams' self-confidence.

Two of the foremost definitions of the word 'image' are:
- 'A likeness or representation of a person or thing';
- 'A visible impression obtained by a camera, telescope, microscope, or other device and displayed on a screen'.

Images shape perception. And whether we like it or not, perception shapes reality. To others, you are what you are perceived to be. A classic hip-hop example: Big Daddy Kane is seen as the oldest of old-school rappers, whereas Jay Z is seen as eternally current, young-ish and cutting edge. The perception is that Big Daddy Kane is much older than Jay Z, whereas in reality there's only a year between them.

So, taking stock of your image and continuously improving it is critical. But what happens when you don't have any control over your image? What happens when your perception, especially at the communal level, is created and buttressed by someone else's pre-existing, overwhelmingly negative perceptions of you and people like you? For Black people, and Black British men in particular, this is a huge – almost existential – problem.

The poor portrayal of Black people, and Black men in particular, is part of a cycle which defines, limits and shapes Black communities in Britain. Below is 'the cycle' in full:

- Racism;
- Poverty;
- Criminality; and
- Poor portrayal.

Round and round we go – unless you're lucky and savvy enough to escape it and stay out of it. The cycle doesn't come in any guaranteed identifiable order. But each element fuels the others. As we are focused on the image of the Black British man, this article will concentration on the fourth element of the cycle: poor portrayal.

Perhaps, to some degree, outside the realm of sports, the portrayal of Black men – both factually and in fiction – tends to centre almost exclusively on the following four themes:

- Comical;
- Childish;
- Cringeworthy/kowtowing; and
- Criminalised.

Case in point: 2018 was Big Narstie's year. He finally hit the big time. As a comedian, Big Narstie is mildly tickling, but his personality is very appealingly. Watching him laugh is particularly infectious, so much so that it spawned a sustained global meme. People would ping a clip of him bursting into hilarity onto the end of other memes in a bid to provoke or signify funny, just like a laugh track on old TV shows. Above all, he is hard-working, persistent and charming, so seeing him rise to success in the 'mainstream' was heart-warming. There is nothing better than seeing the long-term grind of a brother finally paying off.

But there is another side to Big Narstie's success. One that he has no control over. One buried in the old truism: 'laughing with you, laughing at you' and laughing at people like you by extension.

Through no fault of his own (and perhaps unbeknown to him), Big Narstie, a brother trying to leverage his appeal and make an honest living, has been defaulted into the most enduring and beloved of all Black tropes on British TV: the minstrel. The sparsely articulate, physically over-expressive buffoon playing up to pre-conceived wild Black stereotypes – largely for the consumption, comfort and confirmation of white audiences.

Although he has been toiling away for years, Big Narstie was catapulted into the mainstream by a series of appearances on TV breakfast programme *Good Morning Britain* (*GMB*). He appeared on segments presenting the weather in 'roadman' dialect, teaching viewers how to talk 'road', giving shout-outs to his elderly fans, etc. His appeal was clear: he was funny. But anyone with any grasp of history would quickly see that he was 'funny' to *Good Morning Britain*'s target audience in the same way Stepin Fetchit – the first Black celebrity ever – was funny to similar audiences in America nearly 100 years ago.

Britain loves a minstrel show. It is why Dizzee Rascal proved so popular on BBC's *Newsnight* on the sacred night Barack Obama was elected US president, why the original minstrel shows were cancelled in Britain in 1978 (a solid half a century after they were cancelled in America) and now today why Big Narstie has found popularity with 'mainstream' British broadcasters and audiences.

Dignified, smart and intellectually and socially challenging comedy in the Black vein of the likes of *Key & Peele*, Dave Chappelle, Paul Mooney, Gina Yashere, Trevor Noah and so on – doesn't make it far on British TV. The nature of the comedy of Yashere and others smashes stereotype and racism-fueled pre-existing perceptions. Big Narstie's act confirms them.

When we go from comical/childish portrayal to criminalised and cringeworthy, things get a lot darker. For example, in 2016, Channel 5 broadcast a show called *Gangland*. Although it was implicit rather than explicit, this programme focused exclusively on Black 'gangs' in London. It contained everything you would expect to see in such a show: guns, knives, drugs, balaclavas, Black men looking menacing and so on. It also exceeded all expectations for the money shot of the show: a man removing drugs hidden in his rectum on close-up camera for the viewing pleasure of the general public. It was a shocking TV first. To the best of my knowledge, it hadn't happened on TV before and it hasn't happened since.

As well as being entertaining, part of the real purpose of neo-minstrel shows and Black gang porn such as this is to gently reaffirm and reassure viewers of their 'biases'. And to make money – they are, after all, popular. In the eyeball game that is media, where there is popularity there is profit.

These are not the only images of Black men on TV, but they are the dominant images of Black men on British TV. They're the ones that are afforded prime-time slots. They're the images of Black people that Britain is most comfortable with and accustomed to. Predictably, this has had an immensely damaging effect on the real image and therefore standing of Black British men.

In my own professional experience, I have been told to my face – by very senior people in different industries – that I am not 'really Black' or not 'Black enough' because I am 'too well educated, too intelligent and successful'. I do not fit their understanding of what a Black person is. Though their racism was probably well intended, I didn't take it as something to be proud of. I was disgusted by it. This 'understanding' of what a black person is is contagious and dangerous.

When I see headlines of black youngsters being killed or injured in, say, knife-crime attacks, I cannot help but think back to Oliver Letwin. How differently would things have turned out had the Tory government of the 1980s taken steps to economically empower the Black community – an idea floating round the corridors of power at the time. The idea was scuppered by Oliver Letwin because he thought that any investment in the Black community would fuel the '*disco and drug trade*'. Wonder where Eton-and Cambridge- educated Mr Letwin got those ideas from?

The image of Black people, and Black British men in particular, is created and controlled by white people. Often ones who don't know any Black people intimately enough to have at least an understanding of what being Black is really like. In Britain and far beyond, Black men have near-zero power over how we are viewed and understood. In mass British media today, the image, understanding and portrayal of Black people are owned and controlled by the descendants of the people who owned and controlled our image (and often bodies) hundreds of years ago. The baton has been passed down without being dropped once. Hence the cycle remains firmly intact.

The editorial meetings up and down the country that decide multiple times a day how we are portrayed are usually all white and often all male. The group with the highest stakes is the group with the lowest representation. The group with the most skin in the game has the least skin in the room. At best, Black British men are guarding the door.

Owing at least in part to the debasing of our image, Black British men are more likely to be unemployed, paid less for comparable work, locked up, locked up for longer, locked out of professional careers, victims of crime, detained and/or treated in the community for mental-health concerns, among other things – than practically any other group. There is barely any measure of British societal disadvantage in which Black British men are not overrepresented and/or taking the lead.

The story of Mark Duggan illustrates clearly how portrayal affects outcomes. In August 2011, Mark Duggan was killed by the police in Tottenham, north London. But that was not the first time he was killed or the last. Mark Duggan was killed three times: first, he was killed by the media; then by the police; and then again by the media.

A problematic image – one that has since proven deadly – of men like Mark Duggan had long been established in the media and therefore in the public conscience: Black, working class, from the 'wrong' area and, of course, 'gangsta' (a racially weaponised term in this instance). As a result, public sympathy for Mark Duggan's death at the hands of the police was in very short supply. The original official story that he had hopped out of his car and started shooting at the police like some kind of Black Terminator didn't pass the common-sense smell test and was quickly proven to be false. But not before it had been swallowed whole and dispersed without question throughout the media.

Duggan's killing and its aftermath had all the hallmarks of total dehumanisation. Yet this would never have been achievable without a prolonged period of prior priming of the general public about men – indeed bogeymen – who share the image cast for Duggan.

Compare his treatment to that of Raoul Moat in 2010 – a white man who shot three people (including a police officer), murdering one, maiming another (who went on to commit suicide), while instigating the largest manhunt in modern British history. He was treated with far more empathy by the media and the public – a Facebook memorial page attracted thousands of members. Even the Prime Minister David Cameron came out to chastise the public sympathy for Moat.

In the aftermath of Duggan's killing and the riots that followed them, Paul Lawrence and Tony Harrison of the 100 Black Men of London (an independently funded organisation that mentors and empowers young Black people) hosted a community discussion event in an Ethiopian eatery in south London. In order to contribute to the discussion, there was a single request: state your name and your occupation. At the time I didn't understand the point of this. Paul explained it was an opportunity for young people to see what they could be: 'If you don't show them, society will.' This statement hit me hard and has stayed with me for years after the fact.

A Black boy is born in a British hospital today. As the years progress, he will become aware of the fact that he is Black and he will become a man. If he gets his Black-awareness, indeed his 'Blackness', from British media or wider society, as Paul Lawrence hinted and as illustrated above, it can be a dangerous path. Britain seldom lets Black British boys 'see what they can be'. So, if the family and community are unable or unwilling to offer an abundance of great Black signifiers of your potential – of what you can be – then your options quickly narrow.

Whether TV reflects our society, our social order or a post-racial wild fantasy of both, white male children are largely fed a positive image of themselves. A 2011 American study published in *Communication Research* found that the only group to have their self-esteem boosted by watching TV was the group best represented on TV: white males.

My own early experiences made clear to me the benefit of positive images and role models. A large part of my early childhood was spent with foster parents in the British countryside. Just to be clear, this was the British countryside of the mid-80s: to put it mildly, it was hardly a chocolate Mecca.

The first Black person I knew – other than my sister – was a guy who was known with mind-bending literalism as 'the Black boy'. I was too young to know why but I felt some form of natural kinship with him. He was nice to me and I looked up to him . . . until he was arrested under suspicion of being a part of a group who burgled our house, nearly murdered our dog and then helped themselves to tea and biscuits.

I remember seeing him out with his friends not long after the whole incident. I could tell he was struggling not to make eye contact with me, but for a brief second, he did. Even as a kid I could identify what I saw in his face, which I felt was shame. I sometimes wonder about the source of his shame – that he burgled a house? Got arrested? Or he let down someone who had no one to look up to but him?

As I cruised into my own teens, I got lucky (although I didn't see it that way at the time). I was suddenly ripped away from Britain and sent 'back home' to Nigeria as an eleven-year-old. Overnight, I went from having a few TV role models (Trevor McDonald, Turbo B, Andi Peters) and even fewer real-life ones to being overwhelmed with really great Black people to look up to: both current and historic. Bankers, lawyers, Machiavellian presidents (albeit ones who couldn't be bothered to be elected), doctors, enterprising pastors, businessmen, journalists, teachers, etc. The image of what I could be was radically altered and also radically improved.

Perhaps unsurprisingly, a disproportionate number of very successful Black people in Britain today are people who went through similar experiences to my own, or were born in Africa or the Caribbean and brought here as teenagers; that is, people who spent time in societies or environments in which they could see what they could be.

Leaders and criminals, failures and successes, great Black men and broken Black men: none of them are born as such. They're made. They're made by their family, their environment, their society and themselves. They're made by escaping the cycle or falling prey to it.

Of all the bases of the cycle – racism, poverty, criminality and poor portrayal – the latter is the easiest to resolve. It can be changed with a click of the fingers overnight. But it won't be, as it is entirely out of our control – for now. To much of the media, the cycle that black men are often trapped in is perfectly 'natural' and 'normal': it is much more natural and normal to see us in prison than to see us at the managing end of an editorial meeting; more natural to see us in pain than to see us in prosperity.

Until we've found a way to capture control of media, truly diversify it or effectively rival the perceptions, it is up to us to ensure that those coming behind us have a greater image of what they can be and to ensure we each recognise the cycle and therefore escape it – and ultimately break it.

Existing as a Black Person Living in Britain

Jude Yawson

Existing as a Black person living in Britain, a country considered so great, I witness a lack of collective consciousness about our experiences here and how it ties to back 'home'. It is as though we have no content to add to the conception of this country. The famed individuals that have risen through our communities are often hailed as marks of Black success, held up as a common counter-example against the prevailing existence of racism within this country's system. It is easy to raise the examples of Raheem Sterling, Stormzy, Idris Elba and such like to state that Black people are achieving success/status despite this narrative. Of course, these are Black British icons in their own discipline. The aim is to allow representation to seep into the very make-up of society.

Considering society, I often use Karl Marx's concept of the base and superstructure, which represents society as a whole, to understand it. The base of society operates the means and relation of production, which, in turn, shapes the outcome of the superstructure. This superstructure contains ideology, which is within art, family, culture, law, media, politics and more. I witness these notions within society and contrast how we, as

Black people living in Britain, are considered by the majority. It would be a norm mentally to consider the experiences of ethnic minorities in this country if we were represented in those areas. We need to host our history and our art alongside one other. There is no point in museums containing artefacts stolen from ex-colonial territories if we don't teach the impact Britain had on these places, the cultures and their peoples. We should recognise the racist policies of the past and the failings of our systems. For instance: the incompetence in allowing people from the Windrush era and the Commonwealth to migrate to this country without proper documentation, hence leading to the deportation issues we have seen. The media, and the way in which it documents issues surrounding our communities and the people piecing these articles together. Questioning the depth of our education system and why learning about the various identities that make up this country is restricted to expensive intellectual property at universities. All these notions are conscious and subconscious burdens that impact younger generations and leave us with no strong narrative to understand where we are coming from. Nevertheless, the question remains: how? How do we address everything that has happened while living in a society that omitted so much from our lives already?

Discussions on representation have always existed, though we exist in a new paradigm with parameters that can establish something different moving forward. For instance, the interconnectivity we share through social media; the fact that we can learn about livelihoods within moments through these constant impressions of what people think. In this essay, I want to highlight the worth of Black British representation today and add a historical perspective to our experiences. I will answer this question by using examples from parts of society, specifically the historical, social, academic and media spaces.

EXISTING AS A BLACK PERSON LIVING IN BRITAIN

In my studies on Frantz Fanon's *Black Skin White Masks*, I was presented with a puzzling realisation about the Malagasy people from Madagascar. Fanon stated that the Malagasy people were not Malagasy people until they met the Europeans. They were not oppressed until they realized what they contrasted with, the European colonialists. These colonialists had conceptions of modernity and being greater than others they did not identify with; hence the Malagasy people were witnessed as uncivilized and in need of dependence on this European intelligence. In a similar sense, I was just a boy until I realized the weight of Blackness. You overhear your teachers speaking: you are a Black boy whereas your peers are the blond boy with rosy cheeks or the girl with luscious brunette hair. You miss out on a school play and carry a bench for the cast to perform around, because you don't have the skin for these white characters. You mispronounce a word and are a laughing stock, any hint of an accent is belittled. When 22 April comes around and Stephen Lawrence's case is taught in class, it always reminds you that you are different from the standard held by the system at hand. Stephen Lawrence's murder was a tragic case, a racist attack excused by an incompetent and racist police force. Though his is not the only murder spawned from hate crime, his case was made prominent because of the determination of his family and their legal representatives for justice. You start losing a faith you did not know you subscribed to, as justice seems to be foreign. Over time it mounts up and settles: you speak English and yet your mother tongue is missing. You start to build identity and fragments of your parents' identity are extended onto yours. You grow into new modes of thinking in contrast to the white child who, even when considered weird, is still a norm in comparison to your dark difference. The food at school is never to your cultural taste. It can impact on what you are willing to eat at home because of the stigma of being exotic. This innate battle is what many white people never have to consider. White Britishness is the standard we are inclined to be contrasted to. So often we conceive of Britishness through the values and traditions imposed by this attitude.

I recall, before I could speak, 'God Save the Queen' played in my mind: it is one of my earliest memories. It has an enchanting tone and also ties into the sound of hymns that echo in Church. As a result, it gives off the vibe of a higher authority. I felt this link through my upbringing within the Church. Despite the lack of connection to God and the monarch, the whole tradition alludes to royalty as greater beings. Christianity's practices live within this country. Secularised but sold in seasons like Easter and Christmas, though its power extends throughout Britain's and other ex-colonial countries' pasts. The missionary endeavours to convert colonial subjects to establish more control. This notion of British imperialism is evident when watching the Olympics, the World Cup and other grand events and even in jest, as with Eurovision, the idea of nationality and the accolades that stem from the participants' respected histories becomes common knowledge. English also seemed the greatest language in the world. The idea of the Queen's English as a proper way to voice your prose, in a respectful manner like media-trained speakers. Why bother to learn another language anyway when the majority of the world wants to live here and speak English? Hence it has been off-putting acknowledging our mother tongues.

My parents would speak Ghanaian languages, but we communicated in English to ensure mine was clear at school and my studies easier. The TV ads the general public watched highlighted African countries' need for aid. Charity days at school were to raise money to help reduce poverty in Africa. Do not forget the scenes of corruption, war and starvation that we saw which instilled such a poor conception of Black people there.

The news rarely offered any positive scenes of Africa. Back then, I did not want to be African: in the British mindset I was accustomed to, I was too young to understand and maintain pride in my heritage and motherland.

Many of my Caribbean peers dismissed their association with Africa. They had their own stereotypes to deal with. Blackness in general has always been an issue for the racist. Hence my early pride in Blackness derived a lot from the Caribbean culture already present in London and an adoration of African Americans. A sense of Black culture started to rise within me in contrast to the remnants of British imperialism. The notion of British imperialistic pride, obvious in literature and in the art in museums and galleries and public statues is alienating. In my studies, for example, I always had to consider the likes of Shakespeare and Jane Austen, two English writers hailed as among the greatest in the world and the epitome of British literature. I knew of no Black writers until literature and writing were already stark, distant and bigger than me.

I was always fascinated by this idea of the Church and how it is tied into this country. How we adopted Christian beliefs through colonialism and have maintained them without a thought for our prior but now demonised 'pagan' beliefs. When I think of African religions or practices, the notion of the witch doctor and voodoo come to mind. History has resulted in such practices being marginalised and considered immoral. For example, many elderly Ghanaians I know distance themselves from those notions while revering them from afar. It boils down to the educational trail that altered the mindset towards these traditions. The Society for the Propagation of the Gospel in Foreign Parts helped establish elementary education in the Gold Coast. This consisted of Church of England missionaries sent to parts of Africa, Asia and the Caribbean in the eighteenth and nineteenth centuries to proselytise and make British imperialism easier to digest. They implemented a British curriculum in these regions and utilised Africanisation to mark differences between indigenous people. This is how tribal differences intensify. Village chiefs' children and those close to the colonial government had easier access to education and the new curriculum. The use of African languages, as a result, dwindled while the respect for Britishness increased. My father, for instance, always held Shakespeare up to a high standard. He spoke English in a Ghanaian school, taught British idioms and proverbs. He read the majority of Shakespeare's plays and other works and memorised verses from the Bible. He was taught British history, about their kings and queens, about the prime ministers and their parties. He was provided with a European lens on life. These are parts of a standard curriculum for many, stemming back to ex-British colonies. My father and other students were beaten if they made mistakes in school. Many of our parents were subject to such an education and have lived through the causation of events that have allowed us to exist here. It is a cycle of control and effort stemming back to colonialism; a British imperialistic framework that has extrapolated through the times of empire until today. There seems to be a lack of collective consciousness within this country, mainly due to this migration story which the majority of its ethnic minorities share. This story is one so many can relate to. Migrating to Britain in expectation of the greatness people associated it with – only to be met by a lack of cultural or ethnic representation and racial discrimination.

We have been migrating for a variety of economic, social and even moral reasons. The issue for me is that we are not picking up on accounts of similar and previous experiences of people like us, so there is no continuation of them. In British society, these ideas tend to be addressed in academic spaces. I embarked on my own studies at London's School of Oriental and African Studies (SOAS). My degree contained modules on African and

Asian diaspora in the contemporary world. An issue for me was reaching this point, as degrees are expensive. Nevertheless, I managed to learn a great deal on reclaiming space and about the parts of history that have allowed me to exist here, such as the 1970s Grunwick Strike in north-west London and how it was led mostly by South Asian women. It helped ethnic minorities, both men and women, receive equal pay with white workers. I learned about Benjamin Zephaniah, a writer, poet, Rastafarian, who is vocal about his anti-empire sentiments and outspoken on the experiences we faced and face. I read Jamaican-born British academic and activist Stuart Hall's texts, had to look at C. L. R. James and Peter Gilroy, Black British academics who offered incredible insight on what we are going through, but had their own battles to face in their own fields. We debated about Ghanaian Kwame Nkrumah and the public lectures he gave in Leicester Square regarding Pan-Africanism. We learned about the Windrush generation and their experiences during and after world wars. My mind was excited with this pure Black British content, but I also felt alienated and useless as I could not share and enjoy this information with everyone. I considered how invigorated I would have been as a child filled with this content and pride at my difference. What would I have done with this information if I could have applied it to what I wanted to do? I recognised the lack of connection of this information to today and how it was reserved for academic spaces and replied to in a reactionary fashion by the media and government. We should not be reading articles about how controversial carnival is, instead we should celebrate Claudia Jones for bringing the tradition to London. The Windrush generation should not be worrying about possible deportation; we should be celebrating their contribution to this country as a norm in the curriculum and even dedicate a day to them away from Black History Month.

This is what made me respect Americans and their tradition of historic and cultural documentation much more. Today, they tend to process reality through their cultural products to articulate a story or idea. Despite the entirety of their history, including the civil-rights movement and the existence and celebration of monumental artists, sportsmen and women, academics, actors and more, African Americans have produced content to alleviate the stress of racism. Most things during that time have been a necessity, along with many cultural products that have helped build the conception of race we have today. For example, Jordan Peele's 2017 film *Get Out*, starring Daniel Kaluuya as Chris, is an incredible film that ties the genres of horror and thriller through the lens of micro-aggressions experienced by a Black man. Micro-aggressions are the brief everyday verbal and behaviours received by a type of person in reaction to their identity. *Get Out* is even more brilliant as the audience's reactions showed that it can be perceived in two ways. White people did not receive the content of the film in the same way that Black people did in the same audience. The reason being the anxieties empathy allows us to experience. This for me is a perfect example of negritude, which is a collective consciousness on the state of Black or African culture, one which I believe we all interact with in different ways. It could be gravitating to another Black person in a new work or educational environment. Us understanding a cultural reference that implies so much. Or else just by sharing an admiration and supporting someone for being Black. Daniel Kaluuya is a Black British actor who understood these behaviours and perfected Chris in relation to the existing micro-aggressions and for me this shows negritude.

As a cultural product, *Get Out* is tremendous as it sparked a conversation; it was a unique way to propose parts of our livelihoods to be understood. It also showed a unity among African diaspora in recognition of the social importance of providing such stories.

I believe racism is a different entity in different societies. I learned this through Stuart Hall, who deserves to be a household name. For us, we have a checkered trail of colonial effect that has impacted our home countries and ideologies moving forward. It is so ingrained and cannot be undone, just countered with examples that can identify identity. Though for African Americans, racism is much more overt and there has been a constant dialogue on the nature of their racial relations, from abolitionist and civil-rights movements to activism and the social awareness of today. Hence films like Steve McQueen's 2013 *12 Years A Slave,* despite being another slave film that adds another perception on a dark past, offered Lupita N'yongo the chance to win awards and bless countless people with her speeches regarding her identity. She is a dark-skinned woman of Kenyan extraction, who had hated her complexion in contrast to adored lighter skin-tones, but grew into loving and owning it. She reasoned that this was important to hear. It was a beautiful moment and socially her success has added to the comfort of many Black girls and women who experience the same self-conscious doubt.

There are a lot of cultural products stemming from our communities which are countering the unfortunate mental wirings the past has knitted together. *Black Panther* for me showed this as a whole. *Black Panther* (2018) is a Marvel film based on a romanticised part of Africa, a what-if scenario – what if colonialism didn't occur in a country? It is also a unique film that promoted pride, a well-studied African American concept of Africa and a star-studded majority Black cast, including Lupita N'yongo and Daniel Kaluuya. It is one of the highest-grossing films ever – and the importance of having Black children fawn over Black heroes has been paramount. It is in these moments, when such films have been released, that a discussion is raised to understand the worth of such products. We are in a time when we are actively creating against our unfortunate past, resulting in a lot of commodification of those experiences. Maybe if not for the last decade of Black affairs, the international Black Lives Matter movement, the prominence of Black creativity within the pop world, in particular, such products would never have existed. Though there are necessary commodities that have social worth and in the past few years we have been witnessing this in regard to Britain.

My last point remains in today. I have been fortunate enough to edit and co-write *Rise Up: The #Merky Story So Far* (2018) by Stormzy. A British music artist, Stormzy has achieved a number-one best-selling album, *Gang Signs & Prayer* (2017). Currently, the music scene is excelling for our communities. We are witnessing times where we are creating successes through our own means.

Social media is a space that has allowed people to create for their own sake. The idea of being self-made is alluring when you witness a meteoric rise inspired away from industries, instead purely by people power. It is through sharing on social media that I built my writing credentials, and the likes of artists like Stormzy became popular themselves. For his album to achieve the number-one position across several charts and go platinum baffled the general public. They could not digest how a young Black man who produced Grime content could accomplish this, as if they knew about the lack of opportunity he had had. It has been a full circle of a journey for both of us. We are both second-generation Ghanaians who grew up in London and attempted to achieve something with no formula for success. We come from a similar place – we call it ends – and share cultures that only those within it can understand.

The book itself details the journey from ends to the current heights of the Merky team. The Merky team proposed an in-house publishing company called Merky Books, which will allow people to propose books in order to become published authors. Stormzy also has a scholarship at Cambridge where he sponsors two Black students a year. This idea enraged a lot of his fans and people who disliked the idea of a 'racist scholarship', but there is a need for it. The second book to be released by Merky Books is *Taking Up Space* by Chelsea Kwakye and Ore Ogunbiyi, two former Cambridge students who needed to articulate the pressing issues of representation in the institution, of reaching this level of education and still being faced with objects, statues and traditions in that institution that hail from its colonial past.

Despite not wanting to be overly acknowledged for what he does, Stormzy recognises that if we're in a position to help alleviate our position, it is a bad thing not to do so. Hence it has been a fascinating process promoting the book and witnessing us, as representatives of our communities, rub shoulders with others at Penguin publishers, the Barbican and Cambridge University, one of the greatest educational institutions in the world. It is this type of juxtaposition of having Stormzy, an artist the media has attempted to pigeonhole into Grime, present a publishing company and found scholarships, both of which serve as inspiration for Black people. For many, it is absurd to consider the idea of a rapper, usually associated with chains, sexualising women and coolness, actively encouraging people to study and look at this content. Yet this is also a mental long jump over the lack of historicising of our experiences, for this is just a new way to solve our disadvantages. If they realised what this is all worth, mentally and psychologically moving forward, there would be no issue at all, just understanding.

The greatest point of this work for me is seeing young children respond to witnessing the greatness we are accomplishing, to have them inspired at a time and age which never existed for us. Hence we live in a beautiful time, where the interconnectivity of this cause has reached abroad and a necessity has been found, where we are identifying our own stories for the sake of those who have never heard them. Even though many creations and movements may appear a commodity, the fact we are in and creating these spaces for ourselves shows we are not repeating the cycle of entertaining these fields with no appeal to our identity.

Men for Others:
Being Black in Single-Sex Education
Derek Oppong

'Men for others! That is what St Ignatius has produced for more than a hundred years, and that is what you will eventually leave here as. Men that put others first before themselves!' Mr Blundell bellowed over the sea of schoolchildren.

It's a cloudy grey morning in September 1999, which marked my first day in secondary education and my first day in St Ignatius College in Enfield, north London. As Year 7s (or First Years, as we would be known by the rest of the school), we had the pleasure of our entire year being stationed at the very front of the hall as our new headmaster stood above us on the stage, towering over us, while leaning on the black solid podium sporting the school's crest. Almost reminiscent of an ageing judge about to deliver a sentence after a lengthy trial.

'Men for others.' He said this when I first entered the school in Year 5, during a class trip. He said this during the open evening that I attended with my dad. But I genuinely had no idea what exactly that meant for me and the rest of the 1,800 boys standing in that hall. What I did know was that it didn't exactly get me excited about this new journey. I remember feeling like whatever it was might not apply to me or that it sounded like an outdated concept that I didn't have to worry about. It really went over my head because of my disinterest in it. Instead, I had noticed the complete absence of girls my own age before Blundell had taken the stage, and it already felt rather odd. That's how bored I was with the speech. In hindsight, I should've listened. Because in hindsight, after completing my education in that environment, I feel he was just talking to the Black boys. And by 'men for others', I suspect the better term would've been cannon fodder. Because the years that followed were riddled with racial microaggressions and lack of care taken over the well-being, especially of the Black boys, as far as I could see. The environment that the school encouraged was in direct contradiction of the culture and relevance that came with being Black, young and British. I quickly noticed that incidents and decisions made by the school administration seemed to lead to the policing and oppression of students from African and Caribbean backgrounds, whilst coddling their white counterparts.

It's important to provide context for the type of environment Black Ignatians were educated in. Founded by Jesuits (The Society of Jesus) in 1894, St Ignatius College educates boys aged eleven to eighteen in the Jesuit tradition. First opened in Stamford Hill as a boys' grammar school and moved, in 1968, to its current site, St Ignatius College has since then been praised as a beacon school in the London Borough of Enfield amongst others. Rather than referring to year groups with the classic labels of 'year 7, year 8' etc., it used the terms 'first years, second years' to differentiate itself. Even its geographic location gives an impression of it being 'separate' from the other schools in the same borough. Situated in zone 6, along the busy A10 that leads to the M25, it is isolated from all other schools. Those schools are more accessible by being situated in the central business district of Enfield town or along the busy Hertford Road. When my dad first started the process of registering, almost every boy in our year stated it was their first choice in secondary schools and that's not surprising. Very few schools could rival the tradition and history that Ignatius boasted in its prospectus. Even more so because it is a Jesuit Catholic school. Jesuits, or the Society of Jesus, are a religious congregation of the Catholic church founded by St Ignatius of Loyola in 1540. They mainly engage in education, evangelization and special missionary work that the pope would sign off on. Coupled with the fact that it was located on the green belt in the north London borough, our first-generation parents were convinced it was the best school you could get into without taking a test.

Most of the Black boys that went to Ignatius were from areas that would be deemed less desirable than Enfield itself. Tottenham, Hackney, Finsbury Park and Edmonton all had pupils attending Ignatius. Which was understandable. Our parents truly believed that schools in their immediate vicinity weren't good enough. Some were swayed by the deep religious tradition Ignatius carried. The fact the school had been at that location for more than fifty years, and before that in Stamford Hill. The fact that the school never referred to itself as a school but always, in all communications, as a 'college'. The fact that the college didn't hesitate to always mention that Alfred Hitchcock was a former pupil. The fact that there were traditions such as Speech Night, mass on holy days of obligation and a general policing of students that was evidently far more strict than other schools in the immediate area. There were no bright bags or jackets. No hats apart from the ones that were part of the school uniform. (Just imagine those old school pupil caps. No matter how much fashion recycles trends and styles, I'm convinced those caps will never be desirable fashion statements.) No extreme hairstyles. And that would become an issue during my time at Ignatius.

Religion, of course, was key to the college's identity. Each year was split into six classes, all named after saints. And all martyrs, no less: Arrowsmith, Campion, Garnet, Lewis, Page and Southwell. Campion and Southwell were officially deemed as the academic top band of pupils. The classes to aim to get into. The classes that had the 'privilege' of studying the subject of Latin while the other classes studied Classics.

The use of Latin was a huge part of the school's identity. When a pupil starts a piece of work, be it homework, classwork or coursework, they must ALWAYS write the letters 'AMDG' in the top left corner. *Ad Majorem Dei Gloriam* or 'To the greater glory of God'. You could get away with leaving the date off your work or not underlining the title. But if *AMDG* wasn't where it should be on your page, it was an automatic fail. The college anthem/hymn was also written and sung entirely in Latin.

Chorus: *Beatum pangimus*
Patrem Ignatium
Qui lancea restituit
Crucis imperium

Which loosely translated to:

We acclaim our father, Ignatius,
Who, with a soldier's strength,
Restored the reign of the Cross.

Most Old Ignatians would be able to recite that chorus with no prompting, especially while drunk. Very reminiscent of those white, rich, old American men you see at black-tie events, belting out their Ivy League fraternity anthems after having had too much whiskey. Essentially, Ignatius was trying its damn hardest to be a British public school without taking the obligatory step of rejecting the taxpayer's funding. Even then, every family was required to pay a levy of £75 at the beginning of the academic year to 'support their son's learning'. I say 'required' like they were legally allowed to force us to pay it. But you can believe if the school was not given a reasonable explanation from a family as to why they couldn't pay, it would somehow become known by the other pupils. The school was unique in that it was clinging to an identity and tradition that was not only rooted firmly in aged principles but projected elitism. Principles that weren't in place for the benefit of Black boys. An elitism that I could never imagine a Black boy would really identify with nor aspire to be a part of.

The very first thing I realised about being Black in Ignatius was just how relevant we were. I say relevant, but what I really mean was that Black students were socially the most popular among their peers. In saying that, I don't believe that was something unique to St Ignatius College. I'd happily assume that this was the case in any British secondary school with a high proportion of Afro-Caribbean students. If there's one thing I've noticed since starting my own teaching career, it is that whatever is referred to as pop or youth culture at that current moment is usually centred around what young Black youths are creating, but I recognise that this may be exclusively specific to schools in urban areas. What was rather unique (but not at all exclusive), in retrospect, was that there wasn't the classic narrative of being ashamed of being African. Most Black students shared either Ghanaian, Nigerian or Caribbean heritage and there was very little correlation between heritage and the area in which that student resided. This led to a unique practice of 'ribbing' between Black students about how we each represented our respective nations or area in whatever we were doing. For instance, if a student of Nigerian heritage was caught not paying attention and answered a question incorrectly, someone would comment: 'Is that the correct answer in Nigeria?' This would initiate laughter from those not sharing the same heritage and the others of Nigerian heritage would then feel obliged to feverishly defend their heritage (and sometimes this was done by claiming that the student who had answered incorrectly was an anomaly in their heritage). All very much in jest, but what made it rather special was that it was very much an inside joke. It wasn't something that white students could join in on because they didn't have the strong sense of identity that came with being children of first-generation migrants. This was indicative of just how instrumental identity and heritage was to many Black boys in school. It's still something that we do in adulthood whenever we meet.

As a boy's school, it's no surprise that Sport was a huge element of school life. Ignatius prides itself on having high-quality sports teams and facilities. On the green belt of London, it takes advantage of local venues like Bulls Cross and Queen Elizabeth Stadium, while also benefitting from its own private games fields that are used for rugby and football during the autumn and spring terms and athletics and cricket during the summer term.

As you enter the main entrance of the school, you're immediately greeted by glittering trophies and medals shielded by glass frames. As you walk around the school, pictures of the winning sports teams with their trophy are displayed everywhere and what would soon be apparent was that Black boys were very much overrepresented in these teams. They achieved the most and a lot of the time made up a great majority of the teams, whether it was basketball, rugby or football. It quickly became clear to me that this was one of the few ways to find favour and value from St Ignatius College. Being Black was hard but it was a little easier if you were in a sports team. The PE department had your back at least. Those who managed to continue their sporting excellence throughout school were rewarded with various visual accolades that could be attached to their uniform as a way of signalling that they were sportsmen without having to brag about it. These were badges with the respective sport inscribed on it by Third Year (Year 9). Colours or roped fabric in the school's gold and navy colours that you could sew on the trim of your blazer by Fourth Year (Year 10). If you made it to the senior team, you were awarded a special tie with said sport and the college crest sewn into the fabric (another nod to St Ignatius' desire to be a public school.)

Those that were in sports teams automatically became popular socially among their peers because strength and athleticism was important not just to boys but the school itself. Rivalries with local schools were always a talking point. The need to show physical dominance over them was overwhelming. I once got rushed in the playground by a group of my year mates while minding my own business. Enfield Grammar, our rival school, had just arrived, their minibus pulling into the car park adjacent to the playground. They were playing a cup match later. One of my friends who was involved in the attack later explained that they knew that the grammar was watching and wanted to deliver a feeling of intimidation to get a mental edge for the match. I just happened to look like the best person to demonstrate that with. I'm guessing they were alluding to my blackness because I wasn't big or tall by any stretch of the imagination. Such was the importance of physical dominance and strength on and off the field for all that took part. What was apparent was that if a Black athlete stepped out of line or did not commit to the satisfaction of the school, it led to great consequences. If you gained a reputation for being a flaky athlete, there was a chance you'd lose favour in the school's eyes completely. This extended beyond the sports field or gym: one boy was not accepted into Ignatius until Third Year (Year 9) because his exceptionally talented older brother had apparently gained an unreliable reputation in the basketball team.

The unique culture that comes with being Black British is well known for its high visibility in secondary education, the main elements usually music and fashion. I can imagine this, in retrospect, may well have been instrumental in the way my school policed Black boys. I can imagine the culture of being a Black Brit itself was enigmatic to the powers that be. It was, at the time, the counterculture that many young people of colour in London adhered to, and that would eventually become what we refer to today as the current popular culture in music and fashion. However, there was very little attempt to try to properly understand it, and eventually it was written off as something that was disruptive. One of the first examples of this was during the initial emergence of Grime, garage and the Eskibeat. Many of us came from places that were instrumental in the growth of the genre. It was a genre created by those who looked like us, lived in our neighbourhoods and were raised in similar fashions to us. So, it wasn't rare to find a group of Black students in the playground, gathered together and listening to a recording of a Heat FM set from the previous evening. Eventually, this grew into us writing our own lyrics and reciting them over a recorded instrumental. A harmless practice, looking back now. However, a school assembly was called to implement a new rule to combat the rise in, and this is verbatim, 'mob mentality'. The rule meant that if there were more than three students gathered in a group in the playground, said group would immediately be broken up and any repeat offenders would be punished. This was designed to curb the intimidating nature of students gathering in groups in the playground. I often find myself softly chuckling to myself as an adult at how the school genuinely felt that this was a rational response – that nobody in that staff room thought it was ludicrous that children were being banned from gathering together in the playground.

Hair and fashion were another element that helped set identities in Ignatius and was another avenue that could be policed. One thing I'm still impressed by to this day was the ability for Black boys to navigate around the restrictions placed on their fashion. It started off with short jackets. Short purple or black hoodies were made by the now defunct brand Schott NYC. Those would be quickly confiscated if seen on school grounds. So, boys started to wear them on the way to and from school, quickly concealing the garment in their bags inside. Essentially, the real place to show off these prized statement pieces was journeying to school. Whether on the train to Turkey Street or on the 617 bus that took you up the A10 to the school gates. Places where you're more likely to see girls from other schools. Of course, the school became wise to this. Teachers would be sent out to Turkey Street train station to meet students and catch those wearing the jackets. Their rationale that if a boy was in school uniform outside of school, they had the power to police the child. That included confiscating hats and jackets. As we got older and smarter, the fashion became more rule friendly. Duffle coats and parkas were very hard to police.

> *Hairstyles should be short, smart and conventional and be*
> *uniformly cut all over without creating a cropped or layered effect.*
> *• Hair should be no shorter than a 'number 3' barber clipper length*
> *and should not touch the shirt collar. • Hair dye, shavings, tracks,*
> *patterns or lines are not permitted on hair or eyebrows.*

This statement was copied, verbatim, from St Ignatius's uniform and appearance policy which was updated in February 2018. As far as I can remember, it hasn't changed from when I attended, and it's only now that I fully understand just how problematic this policy was. It was not written with Afro hair in mind at all. Something like a fade or level one was and has always been considered conservative and professional in Black culture. But it did not fit into the school's appearance policy. Yet this would've been impossible to enforce. However, what they could enforce was rules against braids and dreads. Hairstyles that were traditionally used to keep longer hair tidy and together were considered 'patterns or lines'. This meant that braids and dreadlocks were completely banned as they were considered 'extreme'. At one point, it caused rebellion among some Black Ignatians.

This occurred in Fourth Year (Year 10). By this time, a large proportion of Black boys were growing their hair out and braiding it on weekends and holidays. But some boys were being pressured to cut their hair by senior teachers. It happened to a young boy who came in with his hair fully braided, along with a note from his mother explaining why he couldn't have his hair in the fashion that complied with the uniform. Of course, the latter never trickled down to other students. This young boy's presence in the school triggered a sort of awakening among some Black boys. That they could and perhaps should be able to wear their hair like other Black boys from neighbouring schools. One boy in my year even went as far as to put extensions in his hair. One white student went as far as to blow-dry his hair before coming into school just to gain favour with the popular Black cohort. Such was the influence that Black boys held among the school populace.

I think my favourite incident was when my friend Chudi managed to get away with his braids by explaining to a teacher that his hair was like this because he was in playing Leroy in his theatre school's production of *Fame*. To this day, I still don't know if he was legitimately attending a theatre school or whether it was just a very good lie to get away with the braids. In the end, it did open a dialogue, though, but not a very useful one. The dialogue didn't include any of the Black students – or any Black person for that matter. As far as I remember, a group of senior staff decided that it wasn't at all a cultural issue but rather a fashion one, and ultimately, concluded that the rule on hair did not need to change and that the students needed to fall in line.

If there was one thing I learned very early in my time at Ignatius it was that not only was being Black tough, it was also very dangerous. One clear memory was the first and last time I reported bullying. I was very good friends with a white boy named Kevin and he told me most things. In Second Year (Year 8), an older boy had thrown Tipp-Ex over his school blazer, pretty much ruining it seemingly for fun. He reported this to Mr K, one of the teachers, who told him that the minute he saw the boy again, he should come straight to him. The next day, I happened to be walking upstairs to science with Kevin; we saw a ruckus at the top. They were Fifth Years (Year 11) essentially being boisterous, so nothing out of the ordinary. Except one of them noticed us and pointing at us out, exclaimed to his friends, 'Oi, you man!! That's the boy I threw Tipp-Ex at!!' A huge roar of laughter followed as they disappeared into the second-floor corridor. I knew straight away who he was referring to, so I turned to Kevin and he had gone bright red and had turned on his heels, ready to head in the other direction.

I followed him. 'You should go see K.'

He replied, 'That's where I'm heading.'

'You want me to come, because I heard him say he did it,' I mentioned, reassuringly.

He nodded. And off we went to report it. I only went to back him up and corroborate his story.

You can imagine most of my peers would've told me to keep my mouth shut and mind my own business for my own safety and to simply not be a grass. Yet, as you can imagine, the school and teachers generally encouraged the opposite, as most schools did. In this case, when we explained the situation to Mr K, he did something that seemed odd to me. He told Kevin to wait outside his office and told me to lead him to the classroom where the culprit was. Puzzled and somewhat reluctant, I led K to the floor, glanced through each door window to see if the boy was in the respective classroom. As I reached each door, I held my breath, exhaling once I saw he wasn't in said room. It came to the final room and I knew he would be in there. I clocked him at the back and pointed him out. Mr K instructed me to step to the side as he entered the room to call the boy by name to the corridor. The boy, who was called Shayne, stepped out of the classroom and into the middle of the corridor. Now, Mr K was a short man so Shayne towered over him. My blood ran icy because I was already certain what was about to happen. My head and eyes went straight towards the floor in a feeble attempt to disappear. Mr K turned to me and asked, 'Is this the boy you heard say he threw Tipp-Ex at Kevin Murphy?' He more or less demanded an answer. I looked up very quickly to face Shayne in the hope that it was a completely different person, giving me an excuse to say no. Of course, it was him and I returned my gaze immediately to the floor, muttering, 'Yeah, that's him.' Shayne denied it, but I kept silent. Eventually, Mr K interrupted the boy's protests and instructed him to see him at lunch time.

The next few months after that were hell. I was a bag of nerves because I knew doing this kind of thing was asking for trouble. I spoke to my dad that evening. He was the type of man who wanted me to toe the line at school so that was a very bad idea. He advised that I speak up if I ran into any trouble. I remember thinking on my way to school the next morning, I pray Shayne doesn't approach me ever so I don't have to escalate it. But sod's law would dictate that not only would Shayne spot me in the canteen at breakfast by myself that very same morning and approach me, but my response would be to make my way straight to Mr Q's office after freaking out and exiting the canteen to do what my dad had told me to do. All before 8.55 a.m.

I spent the next few months avoiding Shayne's side of the playground and on the rare occasions he spotted me, he would simply give me the evilest look. Now here's where it just got silly. I had a lunchtime detention with Mr K in the summer term for some trivial reason. I don't remember why. What I do remember was that Mr K's office was adjacent to a classroom where boys who were in custody for detention used to be put. Which was where I was sitting when a group of older boys entered to serve detention for their own crimes. And of course among them was Shayne. I could not believe that knowing the history between the older boy and me, I would be placed in a confined space with him. Shayne's attentions had solely been on me. As a teacher myself, I now know the key guidelines of safeguarding, as it is now implemented, yet in this school back then, there was a very different culture and environment, especially, I would say, with regard to Black boys. There was an incident that led one Black child to pay for a taxi home because the father and brother of a white student appeared after school threatening to physically harm him because of a disagreement between the two boys. Most of the teachers had prior knowledge that this was going to happen as the father had phoned the school beforehand and issued threats. The onus seemed to be on us Black boys to protect ourselves rather than the teachers and school to ensure our safety.

Ignatius to me was a microcosm of a wider British society. The willingness to accept Black boys when they're playing the 'right' part. Proud to show them off as Ignatians if they make a try on the pitch or bring home silverware. Allowing and sometimes perpetuating the harm that Black boys suffer through racism. Most of my friends enjoyed their time at Turkey Street. But the bias they faced there isn't something they've suppressed. They're very open about it. They say it was part and parcel of the culture at the time. A few even say it prepared them for their future life: it wasn't a surprise to come across such attitudes in the wider world because they had already faced it throughout school. I'm in no doubt that Ignatius gave me my first taste of institutional bias.

I haven't been back to the school in at least a decade. Since then, I've heard it has been through the wars. Changing head teachers more often than Chelsea change football managers. At one point, it was very near the point of closure because there wasn't a head teacher willing to take on the role. But I suspect the school and the powers that be weren't ready to change for the better and be progressive. It's still standing, with a lot of the same rules and principles in place. But now, girls attend. Which, I would've never predicted if I'm honest. Is that their way of staying relevant? Is that the piece of tradition they had to relinquish to survive? Is that the only tradition? *Men and women for others* is the new revised motto. It raises a lot of questions, for me anyway. I'm curious to know whether this sort of culture is exclusive to just boys' schools, all single-sex schools or whether it is a symptom of allowing religion to directly influence state education. Is it something that Ignatius adopted from a now defunct public-school model? Does this new change mean that the oppressive nature of the school administration extends to Black girls that attend Ignatius? If so, given what we know about appearances and the politics of Black women's hair, is it something that can be expected to be more severely policed? Is this anti-Black culture something that is unique and reserved for Black boys? Is the same emphasis still put on sport as before and are the girls that attend just as susceptible to that pressure or is it from elsewhere? As much as I coveted the injection of feminine energy into the ultra-masculine environment that was St Ignatius College, I'd be lying if I said the new school motto had the same ring to it as the old one did.

All names have been changed to protect anonymity

Blacksistential Crisis

Kenechukwu Obienu
Competition Winner

A brief introduction to myself

My name is Kenechukwu Obienu, I am a ninteen-year-old British-born Nigerian from north-west London. For most of my life, I've been educated in grammar and private schools; white spaces, originally not meant for Black faces, spaces where young Black people have their identity put into question daily. I currently study Philosophy and Politics at the University of Liverpool. I hope my piece 'Blacksistential Crisis' will encourage young Black men to tell their story and give way to an emotional vulnerability not afforded to us by society, so we can finally discuss how being in majority white spaces affects us academically, mentally, and even spiritually.

Blacksistential crisis

My childhood, up until the age of eleven, consisted of people who looked like me. I was comfortable, I didn't have to secondguess my identity and ideas of 'Blackness' were not imposed upon me (in a way that I internalised). I truly did not see 'colour' – 'colour' being the frequently ignorant preconceptions people have about another individual because of their skin tone, and not one's physical appearance. If colour were that simple, then I wouldn't have spent years drowning in an ocean of what people perceive Blackness to be, swimming in a sea of stereotypes, and constantly wondering who I was.

> *I used to play Double Dutch with stereotypes*
> *'You talk so Black'*
> *'You talk so white'*
> *Both ropes used to catch and trip me,*
> *Colonise my mind*
> *Mentally lynch me.*

I started secondary school at a weekly boarding grammar school in Berkshire called Reading School. I knew I would be a minority but was virtually oblivious as to how that would impact me. I went in carefree because 'we're all the same'. Ignorance greeted me at the school gates. Some white boys in my year saw that I was Black and heard that I was from London and consequently I was showered with ignorance, 'Do you live in a council flat or a normal house?'

'Has anyone you know been stabbed?' they asked. No response on my side.

People really thought like this, and I pitied them. Keeping in mind I was eleven at the time, I didn't fully digest the situation, my mental stomach could not quite break down the ignorance and get to the nutrients of nuance and the remnants of racism in their words.

> *Heads swivelled*
> *Awareness trickled*
> *My calm black sea*
> *Saw its first ripples.*

My response to racism in my first two years at that school was primarily dismissal, sometimes I would even laugh with the perpetrators, since conformity is often the easiest way to avoid psychological and spiritual exhaustion in these places. This dismissal had set an unfortunate precedent, that it was OK to treat me this way. Once you let certain behaviours slide, people tend to continue behaving in that way; as for the boys in my school, once I let their ignorance slide, they went ice-skating with it. I was excelling in athletics at the time, so I didn't pay attention to much else; it's easy to ignore the world when you're succeeding at something you love. It was easy to ignore the comments about race; it was easy to ignore people invalidating my hard work. It wasn't as easy to ignore the teachers who had given up on me because I wasn't as successful in the classroom as I was on the track (I was by no means failing either).

God forbid if a Black boy excels anywhere but the sporting world. Once my teachers saw an opportunity to exaggerate any minor academic mistakes, they took it and flew it like a kite, propelling it with the winds of their ignorance and gusts of their own insecurities. It got to a point where even I started to question my academic ability, and once fears and insecurities are internalised, they tend to manifest in your life; mine did so in the form of failing grades and behavioural issues.

The words I dismissed
Never did desist
Confused frustration
Coerced a clenched fist.

The universe has a way of forcing people to confront problems they've been avoiding, no matter how long they've been avoiding them for. At the beginning of Year 11, I had a serious knee injury, so I had no option other than to stop playing sport altogether, which proved to be problematic for my identity. Athletics defined me at this point in my life, so it's not a stretch to say that I really did not know who I was after the injury. Waves of frustration and confusion washed over me with such immense violence, the years of snide comments, the jokes, the lack of compassion, the constant hypervisibility on days where I just wanted to disappear, and people, Black and white alike, trying to define my Blackness. In my mind, I tried to become 'objectively' Black so that I'd never have to hear 'you're so white' from anyone ever again, and so I decided to play on stereotypes: I spoke differently, carried myself differently; I wore anger on my face so proudly. I even bought an NWA snapback, which, in my mind, made me some kind of unapologetically Black revolutionary and not a confused teenager. Keep in mind, I didn't even listen to their music. Ridiculous.

Misinterpreted resentment as activism
Unrefracted anger through a hollow prism.

After completing my GCSEs and sabotaging my teachers' predictions, I moved to another school for sixth form. This time it was a private boarding school, Winchester College, where there were even fewer Black people, and where there was more ignorance. Much more ignorance. By this point, I was not angry anymore, my NWA cap had gone in the cupboard to gather dust. However, that perpetual anger that had latched on to me throughout Year 11 had morphed into a painful numbness, about to be made even worse by the environment I would soon be in. Now, I still don't know whether to call this numbness depression – I never bothered to check or see a therapist and for some reason, I'm still hesitant to call it depression. See, as a Black male, mental illness is one of the last things you're willing to open up about.

Anyway, as many people in my situation do, I invalidated my own feelings and went about my daily life, developing harmful coping mechanisms along the way to deal with whatever it was I had going on in my head. For two years, I was just falling into a bottomless chasm of numbness and told myself it was fine. This chapter of my life doesn't warrant an in-depth description of the ignorance I was subjected to, but just imagine being too anxious to go up and get some chicken at dinner in the place you live because not just one but a whole table of boys would erupt in laughter because, you know, the Black guy is eating chicken. Incident like this happened regularly and I felt like I had to hold my breath all waking hours, hoping that nobody made any insensitive comments or put on a show of ignorance. It wasn't the words and actions themselves that bothered me – it was primarily the internal battle I'd go through each time, deciding how to deal with the situation at hand. These types of things would happen multiple times most days.

I was tired. It seemed as if I had to monitor every aspect of my existence just to get by; the way I talked, the way I walked, even what I wore on campus after school hours, so nobody thought of me as suspicious. Sometimes, if I wasn't in uniform, I would take the back entrance to the school library, so nobody saw me and got the wrong impression. In all honesty, my existence some-times felt like a chore.

Craving isolation
From reality and mind
A pseudo sympathiser
Counting down his time.

My academic progress suffered due to lack of drive, but there was nobody around who understood my problems, not even a little bit. My mum saw my report after the first term and asked me what was wrong and at the time I had no words to describe what I was going through, so I just broke down in tears. There aren't really any 'answers' to a problem like this, so my mum didn't give me advice as such. She just hugged me and said something along the lines of 'Just go and get what you went there for, son'. It's not that she ignored the tears, but it was as if she'd been expecting them, had seen them before and knew everything would eventually be fine. 'Eventually' being the key word because immediately upon my arrival back at Winchester, the numbness resumed, but in such an intense way that it was almost palpable.

Eventually I had to fix up. This is not to say that I felt completely better, but I was able to gain some traction and work through this mental swamp. One thing that woke me up and made me feel a bit more connected to reality was the fact that I had a friend going to a similar school, facing similar challenges, but doing much better than I was academically. Seeing him deal with all these challenges so well, with a smile on his face pushed me to do the same. My older brother had also been in the same situation and managed to excel in a challenging and unsupportive environment too, so when I reflected on this, while my emotions were justified, failing wasn't.

The only difference was my friend and my brother were very sure about who they were as individuals and I think that was a major factor in their successes. Moreover, I'd worked so hard to get into this school and my parents were working harder than they'd wanted me to know to pay the fees. Self-definition, to me, was the key. I strove to find some meaning in my own identity and this reflection guided me to *The Autobiography of Malcolm X*. I found such light in a place so Black. This was my gateway to understanding myself, but not in the way that I expected.

Throughout my two years at Winchester I read books upon books concerning race, many with differing viewpoints. Initially, I started reading these books to find one that would define me, give me purpose. Typical Kene, still looking to validate his Blackness through someone else's rules. None of these books gave me that self-definition I was looking for, which was a blessing in disguise because among all the activism and pro-Blackness, there were conflicting views on what's best for Black people and on what Blackness is. That is where I learned to stop trying to define my Blackness by societal standards, that is where I learned my Blackness does not have to be synonymous with struggle, that is where I learned my parents had been through the same struggles and did not send me into these spaces unaware of the struggles I would face. From there on, everything else picked up, slowly but surely. I'm still getting there.

> *Misunderstanding and Petulance*
> *An unaware product of*
> *Black excellence.*

Now I'm reclaiming my [mental] space, and that space is my Blackness. Therefore, I'm reclaiming my Blackness from society, and I would advise people who have been through similar situations to do the same.

Let's create spaces in society where we can learn and prosper among ourselves, where our Blackness is not defined by anyone, where our Blackness can grow and evolve. That is the goal.

> *To be 'Black' I lacked credentials.*
> *Heavy tears like rains, torrential.*
> *In front of me laid my own potential.*
> *Obscured by a crisis, Blacksistential.*

Writing for Africa from Britain

Gbontwi Anyetei

I was born in Africa but left early enough that I might have been convinced that Africa was jungle (not that there'd be anything wrong with that), war and famine. It was my parents, cassette tapes, diaries and letters from Ghana that reinforced my own small memories; I came to know that Africa wasn't all jungle or famines or war. This familiar diasporan wail might have formed the first bones of what would become the skeleton of my work. That I do my part. No young child should live with lies about their home continent. Self-hate and haemorrhaging aspiration that way lie. I have always wanted to change that – to demystify and inform.

So, I start with a story with different ways of interpreting it and with what I have, which passes for a storyteller's instinct, the potential to entertain masses – if not *the* masses. Then comes the exercise in inserting and infusing my personal politics, facts and inspiring African historical facts – all the while keeping it as amusing as possible because I lean toward humour. And all of that before labelling it within a known genre of art.

Spending my infancy in four different African countries meant I was always different. All were anglophone but with varying

levels of economic stability in the early 1980s, and varying attitudes to all sorts of things and different cultures, depending on
how you see the word 'culture'.

Still, I had no clear idea of what Africa was or had been or
what my role was going to be in relation to it. I didn't recognise the Africa I saw on the television in east London. I hadn't
spent long enough in either place to build mature connections
beyond a spiritual one. The various Africas I remembered were
mostly red ground with some grass around single-storey build-
ings. There wasn't war, reports of war, disease; I hadn't seen a
single jungle and there were no white men talking to animals or
saving Africans from anything. Four countries is a lot of Africa
to live in and still move to Britain. That was four African countries that didn't offer what my parents wanted. Neither of my
parents nor other early influences were activists as I understand
it. To me, Africa was mostly this place that had been great and
full of potential and now had a lot missing. I did feel that what
was missing must therefore have been found in Britain, because
it's where we stayed.

Then a book by a Senegalese physicist-turned-historian Cheikh
Anta Diop, woke me up. More specifically, it took the title of
the Diop book *The African Origin of Civilisation: Myth or Reality?*
to introduce the possibility of African greatness into my life and
African genius to my consciousness. I want to normalise that
discovery. Right alongside Africa's non-jungle status, I want
Africans who read my books and see the media I create to be
touched by extension by the likes of Diop, Marcus Garvey,
Kwame Nkrumah and other African scholars who have touched
me in pioneering African genius.

I feel like shows such as the Indian series *Mahabharat* with
subtitles that I used to watch on Saturdays on BBC2 did that
for the Indian population of 1980s and 90s Britain – represented,
included, didn't judge and maybe even celebrated. Progenies

of that show have moved to Zee TV and any number of other subscription-based media platforms. Black British TV, after many 'mainstream' hits like *Desmond's* (1989–94) and *The Real McCoy* (1991–5), hasn't managed that transition yet. Even the US channel Black Entertainment Television (BET) was sold to Viacom, a white corporation – almost before I had heard such a Black platform had ever existed. This tells me that the Black business equation will take some work. Apart from supplying the demand for Black media, consistency is needed for the benefit of the end-user audience and the funders who have to come to see media as the safe bet, the kind of viable investment or useful tax haven that keeps and has kept Bollywood and Hollywood in business for so long.

Add to that Black international hit shows like *The Cosby Show* (1984–92) and *The Fresh Prince of Bel-Air* (1990–6), up to *Kenan & Kel* (1996–2000). These were more evidence that Black shows could sell. But to me, these were Black people behaving like Americans or the particular way Black Americans did. There was never anything on television with people that lived like me or my parents, like the aforementioned *Desmond's*, even Chris Rock's 2000's series *Everybody Hates Chris* and, even later, Idris Elba's *In The Long Run*.

How much of the diversity I internalised and took lessons from back then, I can't tell. It's an ongoing and active process. I am constantly changing and adapting artistically, but my goal remains. Where I am now as a student and producer of film and literature will change annually at the very least, but where my journey started and the core of what I want to bring to the 'game' will stay the same.

Somewhere around the same time my parents started getting VHS tapes featuring the TV hits and straight-to-video film releases from my home country, I started understanding why *our* TV wasn't on mainstream British TV. My people were loud.

Took too long telling stories. And the films looked like the home videos my uncles made with their ghetto-blaster-sized video cameras. Also absent from most West African films dominated by Ghallywood (or Kumawood for films specifically made in Ghana's second city – Kumasi) and Nollywood respectively are any of the deep political and social insights I believe we need in our art. We need the right kind of representation.

We have inordinate Black representation in Britain's negative lists: mental-health issues, prison numbers, secondary-school expulsions (especially after excelling in primary schools) and even in blood pressure, which are all a result of present and historic oppression. We need a political remedy beyond reactive marches, riots and petitions. We need a cultural remedy beyond celebrated castings in Hollywood films and the front page of magazines that will largely marginalise us before and after the occasional award celebration. The problem with African media is clear. Our content doesn't serve the purpose of showcasing greatness, African-centred ideology or ideas on solving problems, and neither is it really an exercise in creativity, with even their biggest fans remarking or complaining about the repetitiveness of stories and actors. With that added relevance the films become more popular and more become invested stakeholders – *actual* investors, readers, audience, funder as well as the owners of houses, office or cars we use as sets.

This is what drives me to create new stories. And in addition to the stories in novels and even in the non-fiction I hope to pen someday, what if I started making films? And what if other British African filmmakers all networked and gave regular seminars to help create more, combine stories and pool resources to consolidate all of this talent to create our own kind of BET.

After planning an African TV empire from London, I've spent the last few years repatriating to Ghana, trying to work out how to start by creating the productions I know I want to write. So,

I am in the position of being poor and trying to put together the colourful and expensive first building blocks of an African Netflix. Even to those who don't read or view a Gbontwi Anyetei picture – I want it known that it can be done and that there's a filmmaker making intelligent but commercially viable TV and films there. It was after returning to Ghana that I learned more about Professor Atukwei Okai and his efforts going from a talented poet to creating the Pan African Writers' Association with its Ghana chapter, the Ghana Association of writers. He died this year, and his legacy lives on. If novelists, playwrights and poets and essayists could do this, there was no reason why a filmmaker and TV-content maker of the kind I wanted to be couldn't operate similarly across Africa's artificial, colonially constructed and unhelpful borders. With enough hard work, it could make sense to approach the media just like Attukwei Okai had approached literature and Kwame Nkrumah politics and economics.

I want *quality* series, film and documentary content. It's quite realistic that we can get our content to the point it is so cool that its popularity is driven by a desire to be creative, entertaining and informative – and better stand the test of time on its own merits.

Making TV shows that inspire my viewers and other creators would of course be a bonus, and to do so consistently would mean that those same viewers, creators and even sponsors come to associate excellent African media with projects they can rely on.

Market success will ultimately be the difference between my original Black content and the Kumawood-made films that blow up off the back of one scene going viral, and critically acclaimed films that are consigned to trendy blipster and esoteric Twitter town halls. My issue with the straight-to-VCD titles that most filmmakers in Ghana and Nigeria make wasn't – and isn't – quality. There's a Ghanaian (probably African) proverb that goes 'one person's meat is another person's poison', so my tastes can't be the arbiter of what 'quality' is. And after all, Nollywood and so on is digested as art and has been critiqued positively in many essays like this and in academic papers, with questions taking on what can be derived from the films despite socially accepted critical merit. There are too many examples of films that have had no preparation, no rehearsal time and poor post-production values, particularly relating to sound. This, in a time when we are supposed to be aiming for excellence, when we are up against 'Paramount'ainous', 'Marvel'ous' and 'InDCent' budgets of hundreds of millions.

Ghana and West Africa's music videos show that it's possible to make the leap from esoteric to international star-makers in a short time. Afrobeats artists have shown what can happen with videos that crossover to music markets across the globe, leading to lucrative personal appearances, features and concerts. But that leap hasn't taken place for film and TV yet. I hope I touch on all the strands and signposts throughout this essay that prove the possible pan-Africanist concept of African media. The pan-Africanist ethos, that it has been done by other communities, dare I say is the logic of a people telling their own stories and the success of our music as a benchmark.

What I do know is there's plenty of room for excellence. Mainstream media has Black men as violent players, fatherless corner boys creating more fatherless corner boys, and Black women as loud and immoral. Shorts funded by non-governmental organisations on the ground in the continent, as well as European embassies and other would-be neo-colonisers have the homophobic, female genital mutilation and child bride, dirty, disease-ridden, corrupt African stories covered. What about some of the stories in-between though?

As a Nkrumahist and Garveyite pan-Africanist, I feel Africa was born in me and has been carried with me everywhere I went after being born. Nothing can be done about the past but we can aspire to help build a stronger, more intelligent, more textured and cultured Africa in the minds of leaders and viewers. To those who recognise what my characters have to say, I want to undermine the power of the media that tells us we're all criminals – stupid, lazy, immoral and shortsighted. I want to write politically without being preachy and sometimes without addressing official issues, but at the same time presenting characters and themes that deal with them or else referencing periods, figures in African history or even folklore where these issues are irrelevant because of an interesting X, entertaining Y and provocative Z.

What kind of TV writing does a Garveyite–Nkrumahist write? How much ideology can one story or character carry? My main areas of focus are:

- Inserting African knowledge;
- telling African stories in compelling ways;
- being at once relevant but also timeless and crossing borders;
- African characters who often don't have orthodox attitudes to the status quo.

I also have a lot of political references – but those will only touch enthusiastic Googlers of unusual names and location names

My idea is to be revolutionary or contribute to revolution in the two common definitions.

1. '. . . a dramatic and wide-reaching change in conditions, attitudes, or operation . . .'
2. A forcible overthrow of a government or social order, in favour of a new system.

Number one – a somewhat 'safer' variety of *revolutionary* – involves being invited to address future-minded folks of a TED X-type audience in order to discuss the dramatic and wide-reaching changes in film and TV making conditions, attitudes, or pertaining to the way African media operates. It is also revolutionary because African storytelling and the telling of African stories has never been done this way before, as I build my Pan-African empire and model my creativity on Jay-Z and Wiley, by making characters and stories profitable in ways that prior wisdom said wasn't viable.

And then the number-two definition, revolutionary in my favourite sense – that is, Pan-Africanist documentary making, film screening, political struggle accompanying a gradual and to some degree forcible overthrow of a government or social order, in favour of a new system-type revolution. Documentaries I am interested in feature stories of African excellence, vision, strength and innovation. I've identified my target audience around screening events and online conversations. I am in conversation with the Bureau of Ghanaian Languages to translate documentaries limited to 'world languages' into the national languages of Ghana in order to appeal to classes of Ghanaians not ordinarily welcomed into traditional documentary screening events in university halls, hotel conference rooms and trendy places. I want my work featured alongside my peers and mentioned in future textbooks, describing how a united Africa can come to be the place that contributes to its own children and the world as a serious continent.

We must organise and unite with some kind of socio-political will, something that links up Africans worldwide who might not always (if ever) agree on everything ideologically. My sometimes ambivalent work can find a place in that process. We must have a vision in order to move forward.

Nigerian scholar Chinweizu, in his book *Decolonising the African Mind*, taught me that African creativity needn't be of one standout kind, like academic- or documentary-style work. Every musician doesn't have to be Bob Marley, every organiser doesn't have to be to the scale of Marcus Garvey and his United Negros Improve Association and Association of Coloured People of the 1920s. As many of our stories as possible just have to speak to an unapologetic African psychology and identity with their audience in the way even the most innocent children's stories from other lands do. Cinderella's ugly sisters who, in the original story, looked just fine but were nevertheless ugly on the inside, Oedipus and Narcissus – Greek classics all quietly reinforce European history, physiology and priorities. I'm a Black writer and not a writer that's Black. If my writing doesn't go toward creating some push-back when we think about what a hero or heroine is – then I'm wasting my time.

We live in a time when patriarchy, capitalism and neocolonialism are the smoothest-running machines of oppression the world has ever seen. So much so that even the most hard-pressed are able to be in denial about what is undeniable. Contrary to popular and unchallenged attitudes, the lines of unbalanced power, the theft of our resources and the denial of rights have never been clearer. When my characters aren't united strategically, they are organised realistically to achieve their goals. They are independently minded, guided by anti-authority mindsets where the authority is white supremacy, white monetary capitalism and oppression. Outspoken characters with dialogue like a 'Black Lives Matter' word slam isn't what I do but a 'Black Girls rock' ethic is, without the accompanying acoustic music.

Call it stealth consciousness or criticise it as characters lacking 'real African' conviction but I like to feel all my characters are pieces of different kind of revolutionary puzzles. In my novel *What Do You Call It?* (2010) and the forthcoming *Is this the Remix?*, Kob's personal sense of Africanness is undiluted by a life in Britain, even after being assaulted by the worst of far-right thugs. In *Mensah* (2017), its eponymous anti-hero holds the law in contempt and refuses to accept life on the terms it's been given to him as ward of the state since his infancy. Mensah is as much a rebel as he is a criminal – a soldier or one-man intelligence unit, part of a missing war. Tal Zando of the graphic novel *The African Line* (to be published) is the privileged son of a corrupt, deposed and dead African president. He handles his guilt and, more importantly, makes amends by cleverly and casually sabotaging the business of multinationals sabotaging the future of the fictional country of Caphasia. What binds these characters together is lots of style, humour and storytelling that anybody can read, watch and enjoy.

Within every ladder of the African experience, there's a rung that will be easier or no longer necessary if we grow up with accessible TV telling our stories – our 'his and hers' stories; telling our women they are beautiful; telling us there are creative ways to make money apart from a 9 to 5 job or unstructured crime.

I want to broadcast our greatness. I believe Africans in the continent and those in the diaspora have more in common than that which sets us apart. If quotes from Chimamanda Ngozi Adichie's novel can be sampled by Beyoncé and British Ghanaians like Idris Elba can become a bona-fide Hollywood actor and star and architect David Adjaye be commissioned to design The Smithsonian National Museum of African American History and Culture in Washington DC, in addition to the in-roads continental African music is making as mentioned above, then next up we can be TV- and filmmakers.

Here in Ghana, I am always pushing at possibilities and bouncing ideas off coders and tech hubs, keeping those possibilities in animation and software-based storytelling constantly fresh in my mind and searching for opportunities to make them real.

Today's unfound pathways will be tomorrow's obvious ways to go. After all, with social media, the way we interact with ourselves as human beings and even the ways of interfacing with our computer-based technology and waste are changing daily.

Black-owned alternatives to Netflix are already popping up. They await a consistent supply of media and sustainable models for paying for and being rewarded for that content.

So, in conclusion, growing up in Britain pointedly showed me how little Black people get to tell their stories in the diaspora and even now in our own lands. The longer this continues, the more profitable the market potentially becomes. But simultaneously the belief that we'll never be able to provide this content grows. Not feeling at home in Britain has primed me for the feeling that I have no choice but to do my part in taking up this challenge.

CONTRIBUTOR NOTES

NELS ABBEY

Nels Abbey is a British-Nigerian (Itsekiri) writer, media executive and business man based in London. His debut book 'Think Like A White Man' will be published on Canongate in May 2019. He can be found on Twitter @TribeCalledNels.

GBONTWI ANYETEI

Gbontwi Anyetei is originally from Ghana, but spent his early years in Nigeria, Botswana and Zimbabwe, before growing up in London. Anyetei has a background in project management in London and is the author of crime-thriller novel, *Mensah.*

JESSE BERNARD

Jesse Bernard is a journalist, writer and photographer based in London and Brooklyn. He is currently a contributing editor for Trench Mag and his work has been featured in The *Fader, NME, Dazed, Brick Magazine, Crack,* The Guardian and many others. Bernard is currently working on his first non-fiction book.

JJ BOLA

JJ BOLA is an established writer and author of three poetry collections; Elevate (2012), *Daughter of the Sun* (2014), and *WORD* (2015), all published in one definitive collection *Refuge* (2018). His debut novel, *No Place to Call Home*, was first published in the UK in 2017, and in 2018 in North America. He was one of Spread the Word's Flight Associates 2017, and a Kit de Waal Scholar for the Birkbeck, University MA in Creative Writing. JJ speaks and performs both internationally and within the UK.

SULI BREAKS

Suli Breaks is a performance poet based in London. He discovered the artform of spoken word whilst pursuing a degree in Law at university. His video, Why I Hate School but Love Education went viral, gaining 2 million views within a 3-day span, which led to speaking engagements worldwide, and working with brands such as NASA, Microsoft, Google and more, and has collaborated with the band Kasabian.

SYMEON BROWN

Symeon Brown is a lifelong Londoner and journalist. He is an award winning reporter on Channel 4 News and writes for The Guardian. In 2018 his writing on youth culture and economics was shortlisted for a prestigious British Journalism Award and he also won the broadcast report of the year from the Medical Journalists Association. Symeon was identified by MHP as one of the 30 Journalists 30 to watch in 2018 and he was selected by the Edinburgh TV Festival as one of the Ones to Watch in the world of television. Symeon lives in Tottenham but supports Arsenal.

ANIEFIOK 'NEEF' EKPOUDOM

Aniefiok 'Neef' Ekpoudom is a writer from the outer regions of South East London. He has spent his career documenting the voices and sounds of contemporary Britain, telling the stories of the nation's most inspired and culturally significant musicians and MCs. His writing has appeared in The Guardian, Noisey (VICE), The FADER, Complex, TRENCH and more.

JOSEPH HARKER

Joseph Harker is the *Guardian*'s deputy opinion editor. He is a former editor and publisher of the weekly newspaper, *Black Briton*, and previous to that was assistant editor at the *Voice*. He edited the Guardian's Black History Month poster series, and the *Guardian* book, *The Legacy of Apartheid*.

ALEX 'READS' HOLMES

Alex is a writer, journalist and podcast host for his own personal podcast What Matters With Alex Reads, as well as the co-founder of the award-winning Mostly Lit podcast.

STEPHEN MORRISON-BURKE

Stephen Morrison-Burke is a writer and poet, and in 2012 was chosen as Birmingham's youngest ever poet laureate. In 2016 he was selected for the inaugural Kit de Waal scholarship, which offers a budding writer a place on Birkbeck's creative writing MA.

COURTTIA NEWLAND

Courttia Newland is the author of seven works of fiction that include his debut, *The Scholar*. His latest novel, *The Gospel According to Cane*, was published in 2013. Short stories have appeared in anthologies including Best of British Short Stories 2017 and broadcast on BBC Radio 4. In 2016 he was awarded the Tayner Barbers Award for science fiction writing and the Roland Rees Busary for playwriting. He is associate lecturer in creative writing at the University of Westminster and is completing a PhD in creative writing.

OKECHUKWU NZELU

Okechukwu Nzelu was born in Manchester in 1988 and works as a writer and teacher. His debut novel, *The Private Joys of Nnenna Maloney*, was the winner of a Northern Writers' Award and will be published by Dialogue Books in 2020.

KENECHUKWU OBIENU

Kenchukwu Obienu is a British-born Nigerian from north-west London and the winner of the *Safe* competition to find an unpublished writer. He is currently studying Philosophy and Politics at the University of Liverpool.

MUSA OKWONGA

Musa Okwonga is a poet, author, journalist, broadcaster, musician, social commentator, football writer and consultant in the fields of creativity and communications. Having completed a law degree at Oxford University, he went on to win the WHSmith Young Writers Competition. He is the author of two books on football, one collection of poetry and has contributed pieces to award winning collections *The Good Immigrant* and *A Change is Gonna Come*.

DEREK OPPONG

Derek Oppong is a screen and stage actor as well as a drama teacher. After appearing in the popular webseries, *House Party*, which gained him a best actor nomination from The Screen Nation Digital Media Awards, he went on to perform at The National Theatre under the direction of Sam Mendes in the hit play *The Lehman Trilogy*. He spends his downtime coaching children and young adults at the Young Actors Theatre Islington.

DEREK OWUSU

Derek Owusu is a writer, poet and host of hit podcast Mostly Lit. He discovered his passion for literature aged 23 - before then, he had never read a book cover-to-cover. It was a revelation that came too late for his university path, so instead of switching course, he snuck into English literature lectures at the University of Manchester.

YOMI SODE

Yomi Sode is a Nigerian British writer, performer, facilitator and Complete Works Alumni. Shortlisted for the Jerwood Compton 2017 Poetry Fellowship, he has read poems at Lagos International Poetry Festival, Afrika Fest with Speaking Volumes in Finland and at the New York Public Library with the British Council. His writing has been published in Rialto Magazine, Bare lit Anthology, 10: Poets of the New Generation Anthology and Tales of Two Londons Anthology. COAT, Yomi's first one man show, has toured nationally to sold-out audiences and he is currently working is his first poetry collection.

ROBYN TRAVIS

Robyn is author of two books, memoir *Prisoner to the Streets,* and *Mama Can't Raise No Man*, his debut novel exploring different definitions of masculinity, being on the margins of society, broken family units and the need for role models. *Mama Can't Raise No Man* was the only book published by a Black British debut male novelist in 2016. Robyn has been a guest speaker at a number of high profile Literature Festivals including Cheltenham, WO-MAD, Bare Lit and Stoke Newington. He is a passionate speaker and advocate for young people and regularly uses his own life experiences to try and teach, educate, and inspire younger generations.

ALEX WHEATLE

Alex Wheatle is an award-winning novelist, writer, performer and playwright. His debut novel, *Brixton Rock*, was published in 1999 and was performed at the Young Vic in 2010. Critically acclaimed novels including *East of Acre Lane*, *Island Songs*, *Brenton Brown*, *The Dirty South*, *Home Boys* and the multi-award-winning *Crongton* series for Young Adults followed. He was awarded an MBE for services to literature in 2008 and he teaches creative writing at Manchester Metropolitan University.

JUDE YAWSON

Jude Yawson is a writer with a passion for Black British culture from London. Most recently, he edited and co-wrote *Rise Up: The #Merky Story So Far* with Stormzy.

Acknowledgements

I'd like to thank everyone who has supported my writing over the years and everyone who supported this project.

Emma Smith, Juliet Pickering, the entire Adegoke family: Yomi, Yinks, Yem and Yetunde, Clarissa Pabi, Crystal Mahay-Morgan, Berthy, Candance, Josima, Moe, Ephraim, Issa, Micheal, Temi, Yannic, Biz, Josh, Ola, Kaleka, Korkor, Sohna, my wonderful brother Joel and my beautiful mother.

Help us make the next generation of readers

We – both author and publisher – hope you enjoyed this book.
We believe that you can become a reader at any time in your life,
but we'd love your help to give the next generation a head start.

Did you know that 9% of children don't have a book of their
own in their home, rising to 13% in disadvantaged families*?
We'd like to try to change that by asking you to consider the role
you could play in helping to build readers of the future.

We'd love you to think of sharing, borrowing, reading, buying or talking
about a book with a child in your life and spreading the love of reading.
We want to make sure the next generation continue to have access
to books, wherever they come from.

And if you would like to consider donating to charities that help
fund literacy projects, find out more at www.literacytrust.org.uk
and www.booktrust.org.uk.

Thank you.

*As reported by the National Literacy Trust